AF552567

ROLE OF LIBRARY RESOURCES IN EDUCATION

By

Dr. Bezwada Ravi Kumar
Ph.D (Lib.), P.G.D.C.A
Librarian
Chirala Engineering College
Ramapuram Beach Road
Chirala - 523 155
Prakasam Dist., (Andhra Pradesh)
(INDIA)

DISCOVERY PUBLISHING HOUSE PVT. LTD.
INDIA

Published by:

Namit Wasan

DISCOVERY PUBLISHING HOUSE PVT. LTD.
4383/4B, Ansari Road, Darya Ganj
New Delhi - 110 002 (India)
Phone : +91-11-23279245, 43596064-65
Fax : +91-11-23253475
E-mail : discoverypublishinghouse@gmail.com
namitwasan9@gmail.com
sales@discoverypublishinggroup.com
web : www.discoverypublishinggroup.com

***First Edition:* 2017**

ISBN: 978-93-5056-854-5

Role of Library Resources in Education

Printed at:
Infinity Imaging Systems
Delhi

Perface

'Role of Library Resources in Education' is an essential part of Library science. We wrote these books as a text for an introductory course in Library science at the Junior and senor under-graduate level or at the first-year graduate level. We hope that practitioners will also find it useful.

Concepts are presented using intuitive descriptions. Important theoretical results are covered, but formal proofs are omitted. The bibliographical notes contain pointers to research papers in which results were first presented and proved, as well as references to material for further reading. In place of proofs figures and examples are used to suggest why we should expect the result in question to be true.

– Author

Contents

User Education in Academic Library

ABSTRACT

In this User education in academic library topic mainly we are giving the information about different kinds of users and non-users and using materials and how to use it. What is the nature of information and different kinds of information? Characteristics of the user and education and how to educate the user. Different kinds of user education specification if user education nature of user education and information displayed containing information about opening hours. Library information rules, Library timings, staff maintained. Lecture methods may be formal/informal, workshop about the CD-ROM, online services practice workshop. Advertising papers, journals, posters, pamphlets.

Keywords: Type of users, Nature of Information need, Planning of education, Guiding signs and boards, Introduction of library.

Objectives

In this unit will be able to understand the:

- The meaning and definition of user and user education.
- Types of academic library users.
- Analysis of user needs.

- Planning of user education.
- User Education.

INTRODUCTION

In information system user is an important component. But our librarians and information managers neglected this aspect for a long time. Access to relevant information is highly essential particularly in industrial, research and development sectors. Right information to the right user can pane way to new directions to research and development. It is imperative that to achieve this objective we should understand the library user, how they interact with the system, their pattern of search and their pertinent information requirement.

Users

In a library or an information centre the user are the last links or the recipient of the information in the communication cycle. There are number of terms used as synonyms or near synonyms to users as patron client, member customer. Of these user is the preferred term.

Definitions

- According to a *'Whittaker'* a user may be defined as, 'A person who users one or more library's services at least once in a year'. Users are individuals who can be divided in to different categories on the basis of tasks assigned to them in a library organization.

Types of Users

The users are one type but libraries are different from those of another type. In a public library the users are: mainly children, student's, housewives, farmers, retired persons, be literates and even also researches. In an academic library the users are students, teachers and researchers, whereas as special groups of users of whom the library is intended. From what is stated above it can be assumed that in the public libraries the users are almost heterogeneous and in academic and special libraries the users are almost homogeneous in nature. For an effective an information service as an information manager should ascertain about the information requirements of his library users.

Information users can be categorised mainly in to four groups, on the basis of their approach to information a libraries, they are:

1. *Potential user*: One who needs information which can be provided by specific services?
2. *The expected user*: One who is known to have the intention of using certain information services?
3. *Actual user*: One who has actually used an information service regardless of whether he derived advantages from it or not.
4. *The Beneficiary user*: One who derives measurable advantages from information services?

User groups may be divided in a number of ways. They can be divided as administratively into internal and external users. Another type of classification of user community on the basis of library service they make use of is the following:

- *General readers:* This type of users groups say for example associated with public libraries generally use light lending materials.
- *Subject readers:* This type of users concentrate their use of library materials on subject field they or working or specializing.
- *Special readers:* The users placed in this group are those with special needs, the result of disabilities of one kind or another physical or mental disability may be distinguished.
- *Non-Readers users:* These are made up sub groups who make use of library materials, but not reading materials. A user coming into the library just for borrows a video or audiocassettes are a best example of non-reading user.

On the Basis of Various Types of Services

Dr. S.R. Ranganathan has grouped user community on the basis of various types of services enunciated by him. They are: the freshman, ordinary inquirer is ordinary reader, specialist inquirer is one who specialist inquirer and general reader.

Here the freshman is the new member of the library, ordinary inquirer is ordinary reader, and specialist inquirer is one who specializes in narrow field where as general readers are the associated groups. In order to satisfy these four groups, Ranganathan has suggested four types of services such as: initiation or orientation, ready reference service, long range reference and general help to general readers respectively.

Non-users

There are certain people who because of their style or other environmental problems could not become members of libraries in their vicinity and make use of the library resources. It is the duty librarian especially in public libraries to convert non-users or 'On lookers' into potential and habitual users of such libraries. These are a number of ways by which librarian can attract such users into libraries by means of extension activities or other publicity methods. The duty of librarian is more important to convert non-users into habitual users and mould them as capable citizens just like other citizens who are engaged in social development.

Analysis of users Needs and Demand of information

The major objective of library or information system is to satisfy the information needs of users. Information needs refer to individual needs of users regarding information, which should be satisfied, by the specific information needed by him. One relates to the kind of massage, in terms of subjects, currency, etc., and the other related to means of supplying them. Information needs of a user depend on a number of factors such as: work activity, discipline and availability of facilities. Information can be primarily divided into type's *viz;* current awareness and adhoc need. In the current awareness mode the users require current information in their fields of specialization or interest. Whereas adhoc type it is need to satisfy a specific purpose. There is information about organization and information about external environment in which is organization is to function.

There are numbers of factors that effect information needs of users that the following factors influence the information needs users community.

- The use in which the information be put.
- The background, motivation, professional orientation and other individual characteristics of the users.
- The range of information sources available.
- The social, political and economic system surrounding the user.
- The consequences of information use.

Nature of Information Need

According to Mellier Vaight information need is a multifaceted concept which is generally dynamic in users. They are four types of information needs for approaches recognised among users. They are:

(a) *Current Approach*: The current is that which users require keeping abreast of the nascent developments in his fields of specialization/interest.

(b) *Everyday Approach*: It's sought for specific piece of information required by the user during day-to-day investigation in the form of fact.

(c) *Exhaustive Approach*: It's sought when a researcher wants to have comprehensive detail about a specific topic on the field of study.

(d) *Brush-up of Catching-approach*: Is adopted in situations were a particular user requires information pertaining to related subject fields.

Users' Characteristics

Lehman mentioned eight user's characteristics that, if evaluate, would help the librarian in his efforts to satisfy user need. They are:

1. Functional reading level.
2. Visual level.
3. Personality level.
4. Capacity level.
5. Satisfaction level.
6. Interest level.
7. Variability level.
8. Vocational-a vocational level.

Systematic study of user community will reveal the varies characteristics of users seeking information. This will give necessary base guidelines to librarians to serve various types of users groups.

User Education

Education is a long life process, there is end. As for as library activities are concerns, the users are illiterates. They need some sought of user education how to use library resources and services. Because the collection libraries are very complicated. Because the collection libraries are very complicated. To know how to use and what the service available etc., is, they must need assistance and guidance (Instructions, Initiation, and education).

It has its own objectives. Broadly it means to bring the awareness about or to guide the users, about library facilities, collection, services etc., for new users this type of guidance is necessary.

Definitions

According to Shahi "It's a process of activities involved in making the users of the library conscious about tremendous value of information in day to day life to develop interest among the users to seek information as and when they requires".

General

"A Process or programme through which potential users information are made aware if the information sources".

Important Specific Objectives

(a) Made aware of the existence of the library, its content, procedures and services.

(b) Create love and books and reading.

(c) To provide the scientists with basis skills for information collection *i.e.*, current, retrospective, date or facts, information whatever it may be.

(d) To make the scientists aware of the different information holding agencies.

(e) To expose the method for strong scientific information collected on different search topics.

(f) To provide techniques for information search from secondary periodicals, reference sources and other data basis like: the online and CD-ROM.

(g) Able to ascertain the relative merit and demerits of reading materials and reference tools.

(h) Able to survey the current affairs in the different periodicals on his own.

(i) Able to understand the time back between the production of information and in its receipt by the user and also availability of various channels of communication between the author and the user outside the preview of the library.

(j) To provide good foundation for the continued self-education by readers by during their life time.

Need for user Education

Tremendous increase in the volume of publication as well as the resulting complexity of libraries and the methods by which literature is organized and disseminated necessitate the user education.

Rapid changes in teaching methods and the resulting trend towards a wider use of multi-media learning resources ranging from the press cutting to slide tapes package and multiple kit. Such format has added new dimensions to the learning process in all types of institutions.

Planning for User Education

Programming and planning of user education programme is very important particularly in academic and research libraries. It needs a careful planning. According to *'Thomas G Kirk'* planning of user education programme requires four things namely:

1. Orientation.
2. Bibliographic Instruction.
3. Course in Literature search and Seminar's.

Kirk has also mentioned about acquaintance with six skills. *Viz;* Reference Sources, Indexing and abstracting periodicals, Library Catalogue Orientation Knowledge, Search Strategy and subject analysis. As a matter of fact many library scientists have suggested many methods for planning of user education. All these may conveniently be grouped in following broad groups.

4. Guiding by signs and boards.

Orientation

(i) Introduction to the library.
(ii) Introduction to the techniques.
(iii) Introduction to the information sources.
Literature search techniques.

Evaluation of Users

1. *Guiding signs and boards*: Signs and boards are the most potent medium of instruction a board of responsible size, with the work 'LIBRARY' written on it should be affixed on the top of the library building in such a matter or it's visible from responsible distance.

On the gate of the library a board should be displayed containing information about opening hours as under.

UNI LIB: Opening Hours

Week days: .... AM to .... PM

Sunday and Holiday .... AM to .... PM

The Library Remains Closed on

Similarly single line boards for self-guide section guides should be displayed at appropriate places. Sample of some signs and boards are given below:

Changing Counter Books

Periodicals	Reference
♠	100
♠	200
♠	300
♠	400
♠	500
♠	600
♠	700
♠	800
♠	900

Orientation

Orientation programme includes imparting education or instruction to user in introduction to libraries, introduction to library technique and introduction information sources. Senior Library staff or teachers of library science impact education of this. During of classes may be short *i.e.,* about 25-30 minutes. Course contents I each of the three areas may be as under.

(A) Introduction to the Library

- *Library timing*: Opening and closing hours on week days and holidays, closed days, times for issues and return of books. Layout of library building floor areas, collection etc., location of various sections, services.

- *Library Rules:* Number of books to be issued according to category of borrowers, type of books, loan period of reference books, periodicals, general books and other categories of books, overdue charges, reservation of books.
- *Staff:* Introduction with the in charges of each section.
- *Procedures:* Membership and registration borrowing procedure.

(B) Introduction of Library Techniques

Scheme of classification, its features, and class number, representing subjects, arrangement of subjects, Catalogue inner form, author, title, subject etc., of the catalogue, how to use catalogue, how to find book with the use of catalogue. Shelf arrangement, special collections.

(C) Introduction to Information Sources

Types of reference books and information contained in this *e.g.,* Dictionary Encyclopedia, Directory of Quotations, Bibilogiphical Dictionaries, Gazetteers, Almanacs, subject encyclopedia, Subject biography, Abstracts, Indexes, several publications, Demographic sources, Standards, primary and secondary information sources use of nontraditional sources.

(D) Literature Search Techniques

Use of indexing and abstracting periodicals, Thesaurus, Citation indexes, Style manuals, how to use citation, prepare bibliography etc., introduction to all audio methods.

(E) Evolution of Users

In the users are examined whether they have assimilated the instruction imported to them. During the course of evaluation then must be asked to locate, find a particular information and put to other search tests.

Important Methods

1. *Lecture Method:* may be formal/informal.
2. *Advertising:* (Paper, Journal, Posters, Pamphlets). If it's limited to a particular small geographical area. Incase of online and database then it requires very wide advertisement through papers, journals etc.

3. *The workshop:* About the CD-ROM, online services (then gives hands on practice-workshop).
4. *Brochures:* It's brought out by each and every industry. It may contain history, use benefits, comparison, purchases, addressee in brochures and leaves.
5. News Letters.
6. Demonstration method.
7. Book exhibition.
8. Display of new arrivals.
9. Mass media.

2 Human Resource Management in Academic Libraries

ABSTRACT

In this Human Resource Management in academic institutions in academic library topic mainly we are giving the information about different kinds Education Recruitments sources. In education policy education, Education commissions, committees and their recommendations in brief dissicussion is given below. In commissions and committees, Indian university commission (1902), Salder commission (1917), Radhakrishnan Commission (1948) Secondary education commission (1953), Advisory committee (1958), Kothari commission (1964), National Policy on Education (1986). In this academic institutions functions of new education policy in the higher education through library. Role of UGC (Universities Grants commission) in the development of academic libraries. UGC academic Libraries, UGC Library staff, UGC Library science training, UGC national information centres, UGC reprographic services, UGC computers and UGC establishment of INFLIBNET.

Keywords: Nature; Selection and Recruitment sources, Methods of selection and Recruitment, Qualifications for LIS professionals in Academic Library, Skills and knowledge required for Library information science professionals, Methods of training.

INTRODUCTION

The personnel management is also called as 'Human Resource Management'. An organization whether manufacturing or otherwise is a human grouping in which work is done for the accomplishment of specific goals or mission. Organizational objectives are most likely to be multiple, as the organization try to achieve several goals and to serve a member of different category of people. In order to achieve the goals, a well-run organization works out a set of rules or guidelines.

Human resources have been defined as the knowledge skills, creative, talents and aptitudes obtained in the population. HRM is concerned with the people dimension in management, since every organization is made up of people, acquiring their services, developing their skills, motivating them to high levels of performance and ensuring that they continue to maintain their commitment to the organization are essential in achieving organizational objectives. This is regardless of the type of organization – Government, business, etc.

Definitions

According to E.F.L. Breach

"The part of management process which is primarily concerned with the human constituents of an organization".

According to Edwin. P. Flippo

"Human resource management is the planning, organizing, directing and controlling of the procurement, development, compensation, integration, maintenance, and reproduction of human resources to the end that individual, organizational and social objectives are accomplished".

Nature

Human resource management is concerned with the people at work and their relationship with in their enterprise, seeking to bring together into effective librarian with respect Library. So, HRM seeks to provide relationship within the library cohesion to effective work and human satisfaction. HRM in library aims to getting the best of the people by winning and maintaining the wholehearted collaboration. HRM includes systematic recruitment and maintenance of labor force, standards, training, etc.

Size

Ranganathan has suggested the following criteria for estimating the size of staff in various libraries:

(a) Number of volumes accessioned in an year.

(b) Anrual budget allotment in Rupees.

D - Number of periodical a documented – that is abstracted and indexed in a year.

G - Number of gate hours for a year.

H - Number of hours the library is kept open in a day.

P - Number of periodicals currently taken.

R - Number of readers per day.

S - Number of volumes for readers.

W - Number of working days in a year.

(X) - X, if x is an integer.

SB - Number of persons in book section.

SC - Number of persons in circulation section.

SL - Number of persons as librarian and his deputies.

SM - Number of persons in maintenance section.

SP - Number of persons is periodicals section.

SR - Number of persons in reference section.

ST - Number of persons in technical section.

Selection and Recruitment Sources

The routine operations involved in sources of selection and recruitment of persons are usually conducted by personnel departments. Personnel department should follow certain-policies, which may look forward, by agencies outside the library. Such active and alert sources pointed by librarians are as under.

(a) Employment Bureaus.

(b) Placement agencies.

(c) Advertisement agencies.

(d) Personnel consultants.

(e) Training schools.

(f) Executive search etc.

Methods of Selection and Recruitment

Basically two fundamental methods of selection. They are:

1. Traditional Methods

(a) *Teacher selection method:* The teacher who knows the students for a long time will select the student. This is selected on the basis of special qualities of the student, but importance is given on the examination valuation method.

(b) *Guardian selection method*: Parent/Guardian makes the choice of the job of their ward. Here the guardian will select the jobs and gives much importance toward the candidate (word).

(c) *Self-selection method:* The candidate himself express his/her desire to serve a particular type of job. But rarely we can find what exactly the candidate wants to do in future.

2. Scientific Method

It is based upon inward talents and environment of fortune.

(a) *Intelligence tests*: These tests are made on mental awareness capacity to grasp things in employees.

(b) *Psychological tests/Temperamental tests*: There are chances that people have a high degree of intelligence and special aptitude. But not necessarily the proper temperament to suit the jobs.

(c) *Aptitude tests*: Aptitude test are devised to find out the peculiar aptitude or special ability of person in a particular job.

(d) *Merit Rating*: Merit rating is usually used in placement of workers in the job suited to their and in promoting the staff higher position. The following procedures are followed, they are:

1. Selection by promotion.
2. Seniority as basis.
3. Ability-as-seniority (Seniority-cummerit).

Qualifications For LIS Professionals in Academic Linraries

Academic libraries depict the changing scenario of the libraries. Qualification deals with the changing educational patterns. The professional of librarianship has been the subject of may controversies in India since S.R. Ranganathan. The librarians working in the academic institutions have been facing many problems with regard to pay scales, status, qualifications, promotion, etc. They may have to answer many questions with regard to degree of LIS profession. This can be regulated with prescribed qualification like the UGC.

Qualifications for Academic Librarian

The following are the qualifications for the post of Librarian, Deputy Librarian, Assistant Librarian, College Librarian and Documentation Officer in Academic Libraries.

University Librarian

Master's degree in Library and information Science with at least 55 per cent of marks and good academic record. One year specialization in the area of information technology. M.Phil/Ph.D. degree in library and information science and manuscript keeping.

Deputy Librarian

Masters degree in Library and information science/ Documentation with at least 55 per cent marks and consistently good academic records. One year specialization in the area of information technology, archives and manuscript keeping.

Assistant Librarian

Masters degree in Arts/Science/Commerce or equivalent degree with 55 per cent marks or its equivalent grade with bachelor degree Library and information sciences.

Skills and Knowledge Required for Library Information Science Professionals

The basic goal in information profession is to provide access for those who need it. The factors that contribute for such an evolution are:

1. Available Technology.
2. Needs of an working information society.

Information activities have been guided by the departments in fields, which require information.

(a) Information explosion.
(b) Collection development and organization of knowledge.
(c) Storage, preservation and archiving the knowledge.
(d) Computers in information retrieval.

Librarians Need to know

1. Technological facilities and resources.
2. Financial resources.
3. Knowledge resources (books, journals, information in electronics media, internet).
4. Broad knowledge of publishing.
5. Knowledge users interaction with knowledge resources.
6. Human resources.
7. Be innovative and creative.
8. Develop reasoning and analytical skills.
9. Think strategically.
10. Possess excellent communication skill.
11. Create awareness among users, mail them accept the changes.
12. Arrange workshops to the user community by inviting experts and internal resources.
13. Be committed to resources sharing.
14. Be an information management strategist.

Duties of College Librarian

(a) To formulate and administer policies, routes and regulations with view to securing the full use of library by students and members of the faculty.

(b) To conduct meeting of library committee a secretary of the committee.

(c) To formulate estimates of annual budget and prepare details of allocations on the basis of last years experiences, market trends, demand of staff, etc.

(d) To maintain liaison with the principle and head of departments of college in the matter of selection of books, etc.

Duties of University Librarian

(i) To participate in the educational policies of the university.

(ii) To formulate and administer policies, rules and regulations for the purpose of securing the most complete use of the library by students and faculty members.

(iii) To maintain relationships with the president, deans, and other university officers.

(iv) To participate in the activities of the university library committee.

(v) To represent the university library, to its users, the general public and in educational and library groups.

Responsibilities of Librarian's

There are mainly seven sections. They are as follows:

1. Acquisition section.
2. Technical section.
3. Circulation and Stack section.
4. Periodical section.
5. Office.
6. Audio-Visual section.
7. Binding.

- *Acquisition section:* The books collection in university library has become so responsive to the needs of the students, research workers and teachers in a university. A selection policy plays a major role in accordance with energy, space and money, for the growth of the university library. While selecting book attention has to be made for the future requirements of the clientele.
- *Technical section:* Aims at classification and cataloguing processes to promote the use of the library. The professional work here is to make classification and cataloguing. Get the books stamped, labeled, call-numbered, etc.
- *Circulation section:* A dynamic character in the library. Here the users are allowed to carry books to home from the library with required procedure. Professionals have made to arrange the shelves according to class numbers, etc.
- *Periodical section:* This section provides current periodicals and their back volumes for research workers. The professionals are made the select, subscribing, receiving and displaying of periodicals preparation of bibliographies, indexes, etc.

E.g., Receive, check and pass bills for current subscriptions, etc.

- *Office*: For the efficient and smooth working of a library, office plays a vital role. The office should not only eater with daily routine but also with future needs and demands for the users. Maintenance of records, ledgers, petty cash transactions, salary bills, etc., is some of the important activities of office.
- *Audio-visual section:* Exhibition of books, arranging listening session of long playing, arranging file-shows, and maintenance of accessions for using projector, tape recorder, etc., are some of the important activities of this section. This section is mainly meant for easy presentation of documents to the user.

- *Binding section:* Invite terms of binding work and compile a list of approved binders. Collate books received from the stack, are some of the important activities in this section. The main duties and responsibilities of all these section are to receive all visitors cordially and attend to their needs. Maintain systematic relation with pertaining to every section for easy retrieval of documents.

Training

Training is the act of increasing knowledge and skills of an employee for doing a particular job. Training is the organized procedure by which people learn knowledge skills for definite purpose. The objective of training is to achieve a change in the behaviour of those trained.

Methods of Training

Training may be imparted through many methods such as: Apprentice system, On the job training, Understudy method, Role-playing technique, utility squad or flying squad method. Educational excursion method and other Audio-Visual method.

1. Apprenticeship System.
2. Understudy method.
3. On-the training.
4. Role-playing technique.
5. Utility squad method.
6. Educational excursion method.
7. Other Audio-Visual methods.

Training in Libraries

In many library schools, the trainees are taken various important libraries of the country. The trainees learn by actual observation of the performance of a particular job in various libraries in different ways. In India, library science post-graduate training is imparted by 42 universities which award a bachelor's degree/diploma in library science out of them 11 of the universities run master's courses in library science also.

Training in special librarianship is provided by the Documentation Research and Training Centre Bangalore (DRTC). The Indian National Scientific Documentation Centre, New Delhi (INSDOC) and the Indian Association for special library and Information Centres, Calcutta (IASLIC).

Types of Training

(a) *Inducting training*: The initial training to be given to the new employees. The aim of induction training is to introduce the new employees to the organization of familiarize them with it.

(b) *Job training*: Refers to the training of workers for a particulars job. It is provided to the workers with a view to increase their knowledge about their jobs.

(c) *Refreshing training:* Through workers are given initial training when they all newly employed. The require further training in course of time, because with the passage of time, they are likely to forget or lose sight of various method, instruction and become outdated. Refresher training is designed to avoid this personal obsolescence in the organization.

Education

Education generally refers to the general instructions about the various academic subjects in school and colleges. Education is the process of increasing the general knowledge of the employee. Education is the process of learning, understanding, applying, and utilizing knowledge for betterment of oneself, other individuals and the society as a whole. Education is the process for thinking, cognition, and acquisition of knowledge. It is confined to theoretical orientation or theoretical learning in classrooms.

Education in Libraries

The Library performs a crucial role in the educational process. It expands and supplements curricular learning. The importance of the library role in imparting and dissemination knowledge has, of late, been enhanced by developments in continuing education, distance education and the Open University system. A library provides the scope for organizing print-on-paper, and other media in a manner helpful for learners. Library provides a scope for student-cent red learning. It increased access to educational access to educational opportunity.

The libraries provide various mechanisms for acquiring, knowledge, and become a platform for conducting self-education. The functions if a library can be stated as follows:

1. Conservation of knowledge resources.
2. Preservation of cultures of different heritage through knowledge media.
3. Information dissemination on a wider scale.
4. Information resource sharing.
5. Information resource services.
6. Self-learning and self-education.
7. Social interaction for intellectual and academic activities.

Conclusion

The human resource management is totally related with the concept of Library and Information Science. Even though the staff analysis etc., are enumerated on management skills. They are not conceptual oriented but also practical oriented skills. We have observed in detail of job-specifications, jobs-standards the size and the structure of staffing in libraries. The selection and recruitment is made on the basis of education qualification.

A Study on Collection Development Books in College of Arts and Science Library

INTRODUCTION

Academic Library System

The system of formal education comprises of three stages: *(i)* School, *(ii)* College, *(iii)* University and library attached to any of these institutions of education is known as academic library. Academic library differs from Public library and a special library in purpose and scope and services.

The main purposed of academic library is to functions as an auxiliary of the parent institution in carrying out its teaching programme effectively the primary characteristics of a good academic library are its complete identification with its own institution. The measure of its excellence in extent to which is resources and services support the Institutions objectives. Library us the most important intellectual resources of the academic community and helps the members of the institution individually as well as collectively.

- For self-development.
- For fulfillment of curriculum requirement.
- For promotion of study and research.

Academic library vary from each other at different levels in may respects but all are fundamentally providing reading material to students.

College Meaning

In USA 'college' is a nominal nomenclature used for institution or higher learning performing the functions of a university. The college is expected to aim at the following:

- To prepare the students for nature living in all areas of social relationships.
- To open up the intellectual horizons both for abroad as also specialised educations.
- To provide attention to individual personality development and acquisitions of skill for a life long self-direction.
- To develop traits for a life long self-education.

It can be summed in the words of the renowned scientist JBS Haldare 'Education is to develop the existing facilities of head, heart and hand for a better family and social life'.

Jawaharlal Nehru once remarked: 'If the university discharges their duties adequately then it is well within the nation of the people' (Report of education commission, p. 274).

A college discharges its duties adequately if it clearly understands what are its goals, and factions in conformity with them. A rich and varied programme of co-curricular activities, which would include: lectures, debates, essay, competitions, group discussions, cultural programmes and contests, study circles, social services camp. NCC tours and excursions sports and tournaments publications of student's journals, educational film shows, conduct of students libraries canteens and co-operative stores and welfare activities connected with financial and medical assistant to students.

College Library

In colleges, library occupies of prominent positions. It is an important and integral part of the teaching programme. It is not merely a depository of books, but an active work ship in instrumental in production of original thinking. The aim of college education opportunities for self-education to the deserving and enthusiastic students with any distinction.

These libraries developed in each student a sense of responsibility in the pursuit of knowledge, college library simulates the students to obtain evaluate and recognize knowledge and to familiarize him self with the trends of knowledge for further education and learning new disciplines.

Objectives of College Library

The objectives should be that a college library should become an instrument of instruction. In order to determine, how for it has succeed in achieving the objective, one should determine the extent to which the users use the resources of the library as an integral part of the curriculum in other words it means that teaching in the classroom must depend more on library than the text books. That is library must become an integral part of teaching programme. A college library has the following objectives.

- To promote the records of human knowledge and to keep them upto date in accordance with the growing needs and requirements of users of today and tomorrow.
- To provide individual and group guidance to the readers in the user library resources with practical demonstration on how to procure information.
- To furnish the students the background material on the work to be done in the class and laboratory and this supplement the instructional programme of the college.
- To make the students confident enough to comport and overcome any problem, mental, move or otherwise and to take a positive view of life.
- To encourage the students to develop skills for self education and to introduce them to various types of documents and other media which may sharpen their memory and intellect of many contribute to their personal development.
- To assist the teaching staff in organizing the synthetic method of teaching.

- To keep the teaching staff abreast of the latest developments in the fields of their interests and emergence of new subject related to the field pf their study and research.

The objectives should be that a college library should become an instrument of instruction. In order to determine, how far it has succeeded in achieving the objectives, one should determine the extent to which users (students and faculty) use the resource of the library as an integral part of the curriculum. In other words it means that teaching in the classroom must depend more on the library that the text books. That is library must become an integral of teaching programme.

In USA, the concept of 'Library-College' has been used successfully. The college is considered a library is regarded as a college. The education becomes student centered and encourages students to play a dynamic creative note in their own education. The effectiveness of student-learning process is increased by various means especially the use of library centre students are expected to do independent study with guidance from teachers, who are expects in bibliographical organization. Libraries having suitable qualifications and experience can also provide guidance.

It may be added that the major distinction between college library and University library lies lays emphasis upon providing for the needs of researches.

Function of College Library

A College library is expected to support the objectives of the college thus the basic function of a college library is to assist its parent body to carry out its progamme. This means that it must adequately serve the needs and requirements of the teachers and students towards reading, study and research. This can be achieved if facilities and services are made available towards this end. It may be added that the major distinction between a college library and university library lies in the fact that a university library lays emphasis upon providing for the needs of researchers.

Library Resources

In most of the colleges, teaching is examination-oriented based on 'teacher-classroom' approach. Present day philosophy of education is that teaching should be student resources centered. The concept of resources is concerned with the inclusion of documents such as: tape records, video and audio cassettes, gramophone records, microfilms, maps etc., thus according to this approach, a college library is expected not only to acquire traditional types of documents but also a variety of new instructional aids.

Responsibilities of Librarian and Staff

A college librarian would be the only professional working in the library. Therefore the librarian will be responsible for all professional jobs concerned with selection, acquisition, processing of documents. The success of college library will greatly depend upon the capability of the librarian. Staffing is one of the important areas of management. Which is now popularly called as personnel management or human resource management?

Staff of any library can be of four types namely.

1. Professional.
2. Semi-professional.
3. Non-professional.
4. Technical.

Professional staff consists of persons having degree of postgraduate degree in Library and Information science. Such a staff member can handle the library work independently by accepting responsibility. Librarian, Deputy Librarian, Assistant Librarian in a college can be included in this group. Semi professional staff in a group of persons who are appointed as library assistants and library attendants. These persons generally possess diploma or certificate in library and information science.

Non-professional or the supporting staff members who perform the administrative jobs like: typing, accounts, clerk, peon and they can be included in this category. In addition to the categories of staff cited above, a library requires some technical persons too. Libraries possess information sources like: films, cassettes, micro films transparencies, floppies and such other audiovisuals. A library must have Xerox reprographic facilities. To operate these machines, one requires operators. Such operators of various machines can be included under technical staff required for the library.

The job description is necessary to analyze the various jobs and procedures in the library. This is called job analysis. Further it is to be decided that how much work is to be done and how much staff is required for it. Time at motion study is sometimes used for this purpose. However, the study could not be carried out for all jobs in the library. There are various service points where a minimum number of persons are to be provided without calculation of jobs, that is property counter, reading room, circulation desk etc.

Services of College Library

Services in College Library can be grouped under two heads.

1. Core Services.
2. Desirable Services.

Core Services

- Library is to be kept open at least twelve hours a day.
- However, if the hours teaching are more, college library is to be kept open two hours after these timings.
- Reading room of the library is to be kept open on Sundays and holidays except during the last days of summer vacation and immediately after it.
- Students should be able to borrow minimum of two and maximum five books at a time from the library.
- The library should display regularly important articles appearing in newspapers, which will be useful for students.

- A separate section of current awareness services is to be made available in a college library where the useful information is stored and displayed.
- Librarian should constantly keep in touch with changes in curriculum and in other educational environment and design services, which will ensure library's contribution in the activities of the college.

Desireable Services

- Library can provide SDI services for the teachers to keep their knowledge up to date.

To ıender obtrusive service such as: providing vital items of information, which will be useful for students in building up their general knowledge? Some of the activities in this category that can be undertaken are:

(a) Occasional exhibitions of documents.

(b) Information about scholarship, free ships.

(c) Advertising for recruitment and career guidance information.

(d) Exhibition and display of collection of local interest including documents written by local persons.

(e) Internet connectively facility.

(f) Helping the students for complete of their project work.

(g) Preparation of bibliographies, either asked or unasked.

(h) Helping the students for essay, quiz competitions.

(i) Helping the readers for preparation of talks on radio, television, Public Speaking etc.

(j) Display of writings appeared in periodicals, newspapers, written by the Students.

(k) Extending library facility to past students.

(l) Starting library facility for the students registered external students from examination by accepting deposit and fee for it.

Collection

The college library collection is mainly limited to books and periodicals. The modern media such as: taps, slides, films etc., are not available in large majority of the colleges. The only non-book materials found available in almost all colleges are maps. Most of the colleges are acquiring books on the basis of the syllabus including books suggested for reading a reference of the courses offered. A separate text book collection and book bank is also maintained by college libraries.

Use of College Library

Level and extent of the use a college library would largely depend upon the following:

- Collection of the library.
- Services provided by library.
- Type of curriculum.
- Methods of teaching followed by faculty.
- Attitudes of the faculty towards role of library in teaching-learning process.

The following levels of library use: Text book level use co curricular level use, independent level use, research level use.

In Indian college libraries, text book level use depends upon quality of predominant one. Co-curricular level use depends upon quality of teaching and level of students. Research level us is carried out by some of the colleges on a small scale by teachers. This level of use of is likely to increase in the years to come due to incisive being provided to the teachers to go for research degrees.

Processing

In college libraries usually Dewey decimal classification is used. Many of the libraries use colon classification. Special college libraries prefer to adopt universal decimal classification. In order to decide choice for a scheme of classification, one should choose a scheme which is likely to meet the requirements of the users to a maximum extent.

Indian college libraries use either Anglo-American cataloguing rules (1967) or Dr. S.R. Ranganathan's classified catalogue code 5th edition 1964. Most of the college libraries prefer dictionary catalogue. Anglo-American catalogue rules is preferred, it may be added that every few college library prepared subject headings.

Users of College Library

The uses of the college library are the teachers and mostly undergraduate student sand P.G. Diploma course students. For U.G. students there is a need for initiation and instruction so that they are able to locate and search for the documents independently, the students who join the college in the first year should be invited to come to the library in groups for initiation or orientation programme. They should be shown round the library and the entire library produces and practice should be explained to them so that they do not feel shy of coming to the library.

The students generally come to the library for study of textbooks and for completion of their assignments given to them from time to time. For this purpose, the reference librarian must offer assistance to them. The student should be guided how to consult the catalogue and locate the book of the author or title or subject of the book is known. The various sequences in which the reading material is arranged should also be explained to them; so that he comes to know there the books of his interest will be available. For fulfillment of their assignments the use indexed, bibliographies and other reference tool should be made known to them. Even then, if any assistance in location or searching for the document is required. The reference librarian should help him. There should also be the provision of reader's advisory service.

The reference librarian should also be helpful to teachers. If the material is not available in the library, that should be obtained on inter-library loan from other libraries. Generally the college libraries are manned by 1 to 2 library professionals. If the time and resources permit, the bibliographies, in the subjects of interest to the faculty members for their research should be prepared, Though very costly books and journals out of print materials and rare materials and specialized literature are scarcely available in college libraries, but the collection of the college library must be geared towards the instructional programme of the college and incase of text books, if the funds permit, multiple copies should be purchased for the benefit to the students and the teachers. Apart from the books covering all areas pertaining to their curriculum, some journals and all references collections of the introductory level will be required. The aim should be to promote and supplement college teaching.

For any new assignments to the students and for every new topic the teacher and the reference is able to provide the material useful for the students. The reference librarian should be freely accessible tot he students. He should be prepared to provide factual information himself when its most important to the user, but the reference librarian not get himself involved in doing the students work for them.

At present good reference service in college libraries in India is missing to a large extent. The ways and means must be found that there is greater use of library among the college going students. Necessary reforms in methods of teaching and examination are also required. References for various topics of study and assignments should be given to students frequently to enable them to draw upon the resources of the library and promote their reading habits. It also been suggested that if an elective course in the use of books and library is not possible to be introduced, some topics pertaining to library and its use, should be included in the general prose text books for the students.

Books Section in College Library

A library is judged not by the volume it possesses but by the variety and quality of the books. The responsibility falls on the following person.

1. Librarian.
2. Library committee.
3. Faculty.

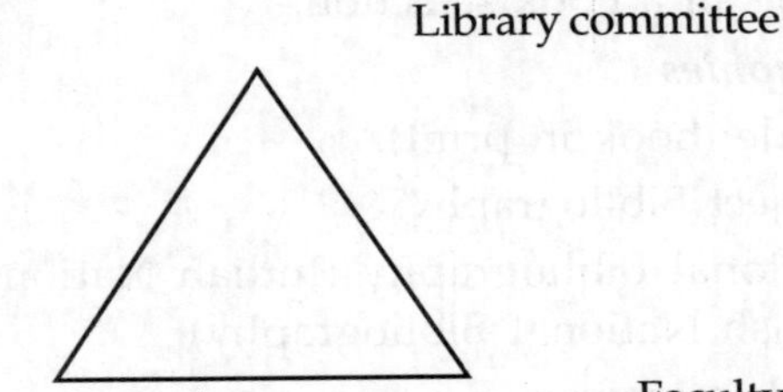

Books Elections follow any One of the following Theories

- Dewey's motto 'The best reading for the largest number at the least cost'.
- Mccolvin's Demand Theory Demand for books should be differentiated according to value, variety and volume of books.
- Drury's principle-to provide right book to the right reader.

It is the college librarian duty to provide a well balanced collection having in mind the type for users and the availability of funds.

Sources of Book Selection

- The librarian in order to provide four categories of reading material.
- Reference material.
- Curriculum material.
- General material.
- Research materials has to rely on.

Human source which comprise the following subject specialist

- Heads of the departments.
- Research scholars.
- Library users.

Documentary sores include trade lists, bibliographies, secondary periodicals, Government publications and syllabi of various courses.

4. Tools of a book selection.

Bibliographies

- Trade (book in print).
- Subject Bibliography.
- National Bibliography (Indian National Bibliography, British National Bibliography).
- Book reviews.
- Book on approval.
- Book ordering.

Tools of Periodicals Selection

- Union list of serials.
- Ulrich International periodical directory.
- Directory of Indian Scientific periodicals.
- Reader's Guideto periodical literature.
- Guide to Indian periodical literature.
- Review of journals.

Automation in College Libraries

For easy functioning, accuracy, economy in human labor, money and time, promptness in service, the house keeping operations are performed effectively to control over and improve the entire operations. Circulation control is one of the most wisely automate library operation, and it often the first activity that libraries consider automating, user identification number assigned for ever individual is types for each transaction, for effective circulation control system.

The following services-computer based information services provided.

Indexing, abstracting of documents, SDI, CAS to provide online catalogue services, searching and providing printouts of relevant information *e.g.* LISA (Library and information science abstract in CD-ROM).

Network of Libraries

In National information system, Information and library network is a compute communication network lining libraries, academics and research community across the country.

The participation in the network will cover the following Universities/institutions of higher learning covering all disciplines, R&D institutions and national organization in the country which are like: CSIR, ICAR, ICMR, ICSSR, DOT, DOE, etc.

Network information Nodes covers the following information nodes-regional centers, University library college/Departmental libraries, sect oral information centers, document resources centers.

College and department libraries will maintain their own library catalogue of monographs, serials and non-book material and will feed catalogue information of existing holdings as well as new addition to UI.

Place of College Library in Education

The college library has been described by various by various educationist as the 'Never center of the Institution', 'Apex of the elective academic lfic', 'Temple of learning' and 'Head and Heart of the educational institution' etc.

A college sharpens the intellectual and develops talents to teachers how to the live successfully in the society. It enables the students to be responsive and responsible to the problems faced by the contemporary society and motivates them to contribute to the welfare of their fellow beings.

The college library assures important role in the process of college education. It is the heart in an academic institution with arteries running into all its departments. The students who receive education in the institutions where libraries effective service come out with wholesome personality, civic sense and contribute to the democratic process in the country.

The college library encourages and fulfills the needs and requirements of an individual. The learning which takes place in a classroom or laboratory is supplemented by a variety of reading materials. The library inculcates the habit of reading and develops love for books among students.

The quality of teaching and learning process depends on the resources of the college library and the library staff being alert and active in dissemination of the new knowledge.

Factors that bring Vitality to College Library

- Physical facilities.
- Reading resources.
- Library fiancé.
- Reader services.
- Library personnel.
- Teaching methods.
- Examination system.
- Library minded management.
- Modernization.

College libraries are evaluated for knowing how far they are meeting their goals, for making decision and also for allocation of rends. A large number of students do not come up because of full of higher education. Motivation is a power which crates a desire in a person to do certain work.

Therefore, it's essential to motivate the students to use the college library and also to make the library service more responsible to their needs. This will help in bringing qualitative chance the lives of out future citizens. The investigator made a study about the use of the library materials Theni College of Arts and Science Library.

Results and Discussion

Distribution of Total Number of Users (Students)

The total number student users of library are classified as UG under graduates, Diploma. The UG, PG, Diploma further classified on the basis of year of study as I year, II year, III year.

The distribution of users (students) is given in the following Table 3.1.

Table 3.1: Users of Library (Students)

Year	UG	Percentage	PG Diploma	Percentage
I Year	340	34.7%	282	47%
II year	172	33.74%	-	-
III year	117	31.97%	-	-
	629	100%	-	-

Table 3.1 shows that in both UG and PG Diploma the number of users are more in the I year with UG students of 34.27 per cent and PG Diploma students of 47 per cent.

The students joining under graduate courses are to be provided with adequate introduction of the library and it's important in their studies.

Through the post graduates are aware of the general techniques of the library use, there is a need for training them in the use of library for the specialized field or topic of a subject.

Table 3.2: Chi-square Test for Users of Library (Students)

Observed Frequency (O)	Expected Frequency (E)	(O-E)	$(O-E)^2$	$(O-E)^2E$
34.27%	100%	-65.73%	4320.43	43.20
33.74%	100%	-66.26%	4390.38	43090
31.97%	100%	-68.03%	4628.08	463.28
47%	100%	-53%	2809	28.09
43.17%	100%	-56.83%	3229.64	32.29
9.83%	100%	-90.17%	8130.62	81.30 275.06

The Chi-square test shows that the users of library respondents are 275.06.

Distribution of Total Number of Users (Staff)

The total numbers of staff are users of library and classified as Teaching staff and Non-Teaching staff and they are further classified on the basis of the Departments to which they belong. The distribution of users (staff) is given in the following Table 3.3.

Table 3.3: Users of Library (Staff)

Department	Teaching Staff	Non-Teaching Staff	Total	Percentage
Tamil	9	-	-	6%
English	14	-	14	4.70%
Mathematics	13	-	13	4.36%
Commerce	13	5	18	6.04%
Economics	15	5	20	6.7%
Computer Science	23	6	29	9.73%
Library	1	5	6	2.01%
Physical Education	2	-	2	0.67%
Biotechnology	10	3	13	4.36%

Table 3.3 shows that the number of users are more in the other category of Non-Teaching staff of about 101 and with regard to Teaching staff it is the staff of computer science department of about 23.

Table 3.3 also shows that the total number of teaching staff is 161 and that of Non-teaching staff are 137 and total number of staff is 298.

The Chi-Square test shows for the users of library (Staff) are 1510.04.

Distribution of Library Materials – Books Acquired by the Library

Here the Numbers of Library Materials – Books which are Purchased are Given According to Year of Acquisition.

Table 3.4: Chi-square Test for Users of Librry (Staff)

Observed Frequency (O)	Expected Frequency (E)	(O-E)	$(O-E)^2$	$(O-E)^2E$
6%	100%	-94%	8886	88.36
4.70%	100%	-95.3%	9082.09	90.82
4.36%	100%	-95.64%	9147.00	91.47
5.70%	100%	-94.3%	8892.49	88.92
6.04%	100%	-93.96%	8828.48	88.28
6.04%	100%	-93.96%	8828.48	88.28
6.7%	100%	-93.3%	8704.89	87.04
4.36%	100%	-95.64%	9147.00	91.47
9.73%	100%	-90.27%	8148.67	81.48
2.01%	100%	-97.99%	9602.04	96.02
0.67%	100%	-99.33%	9866.44	98.66
4.36%	100%	-95.64%	9147.00	91.47
2.68%	100%	-97.32%	9471.18	94.74
1.34%	100%	-98.66%	9733.79	97.33
1.34%	100%	-98.66%	9733.79	97.33
2.01%	100%	97099%	9602.04	96.02
34.9%	100%	-65.1%	4238.01	42.38
				1510.04

The distribution of library material acquired is given in the following Table 3.5.

Table 3.5:

Year	Total No. of Books Acquired	Percentage
2001	2043	11.37%
2002	3058	17.02%
2003	3144	17.50%
2004	3820	.21.26%
2005	3811	21.21%
2006	2093	11.65%
		100%

Table 3.5 shows that total number of books purchased in 2001 is 2043 which comprise of 11.3 per cent and that of 2001 is 3820 which is 21.26 per cent.

Table 3.6: Chi-square Test for Yearwise Acquisition of Books

Year	Observed Frequency (O)	Expected Frequency (E)	(O-E)	$(O-E)^2$	$(O-E)^2E$
2001	11.37%	100%	-86.63	7855.27	78.55
2002	17.02%	100%	-82.98	6885.68	68.86
2003	17.50%	100%	-82.5	6806.25	68.06
2004	21.26%	100%	-8.78	6199.98	61.99
2005	21.21%	100%	-78079	6207.86	62.08
2006	11.65%	100%	-88.35	7805.72	78.06
					417.60

The Chi-Square test shows for the year wise acquisition of books are 417.60.

Distribution of Libray Materials Books According to their Subjects

Here the total collections of library materials-books are classified according to the subjects. The total number of books in each subject is given.

The distribution of library materials-books according to the subject is given in the following Table 3.7.

Table 3.7: Subject-wise Numbers of Books

Subject	Total No. of Books	Percentage
Book Bank	4147	15.71%
Tamil	1435	5.25%
Mathematics	2341	8.56%
General	1578	5.77%
Spoken English	86	0.31%
Bio-Tech	2271	8.30%
Computer Science	3295	12.06%
Economic	4421	16.185%
Self Development	38	0.14%
English	1514	5.54%

Table 3.7 shows that of the total collection of 27331, the books which belong to subject Tamil has the highest percentage about 16.18 per cent and that of lowest percentage of self-development books about 0.14 per cent.

Table 3.8: Chi-square Test for Subject-wise Number of Books

Observed Frequency (O)	Expected Frequency (O)	(O-E)	$(O-E)^2$	$(O-E)^2E$
15.17%	100%	-84.83	7196.12	71.96
5025%	100%	-94.75	8977.56	89.78
8.56%	100%	-91.44	8361.27	83.51
5.77%	100%	-94.23	8879.29	88.79
0.31%	100%	-99.69	9938.09	99.38
2.04%	100%	-97.96	9596.16	95.96
8.30%	100%	-91.7	8408.89	84.08
12.06%	100%	-87.94	7733.44	77.33
16.18%	100%	-83.82	7026.63	70.26
0.14%	100%	-99.86	9972.01	99.72
5.54%	100%	-94.46	8922.69	89.22
4.47%	100%	-95.53	9125.98	91.25
2.13%	100%	-97.87	9578.53	95.79
1.67%	100%	-98.93	9787.14	97.87
5.99%	100%	-94.01	8837.88	88.37
6.98%	100%	-93.02	8652.72	86.52
				1409.89

The Chi-Square test shows that the subject-wise number of books is 1404.89.

Distribution of Library Materials-periodicals

Here the periodicals are classified according to the publication as Indian and Foreign and are further classified as Journals, Magazines, and other periodicals.

The distribution of library materials-periodicals is given in the following Table 3.9.

Table 3.9: Total Numbers of Periodicals

Periodical	Indian	Foreign	Total	Percentage
Journals	90	13	103	50.74%
Magazines	72	7	79	38.92%
Other Periodicals	21	-	21	10.34%
Total	183	20	202	100%

Table 3.9 shows that 90 Indian Journals, 13 Foreign Journals and a total of 103 comprises of highest percentage of about 50.74 per cent.

Table 3.10: Chi-square Test for Total Number of Periodicals

Observed Frequency (O)	Expected Frequency (E)	(O-E)	$(O-E)^2$	$(O-E)^2E$
50.74%	100%	-49.26%	2426.54	24.26
38.92%	100%	-61.08%	3730.76	37.31
10.34%	100%	-89.66%	9038.91	80.38 141.95

The Chi-Square test shows that the total number periodicals are 141.95.

Distribution of Library Materials – Journals According to their Subjects

Here the total collection of library materials-journals is classified according tot he subjects. The total number of journals in each subject is given. The distribution of library materials-journals according to the subject is given in the following Table 3.11.

Table 3.11 shows that of the total collection of 103 journals the journals which belong to subject English as the highest percentage of about 12.62 per cent and that of lowest percentage journals of Biochemistry of about 3.88 per cent.

Table 3.11: Subject-wise Numbers of Journals

Subject	No. of Journals	Percentage
English	13	12.62%
Tamil	7	6.80%
Economic	10	9.71%
Mathematics	10	9.71%
Commerce	12	11.65%
Computer Science	11	10.68%
General	10	9.71%
Total	103	100

Table 3.12: Chi-sqare Test for Subject-wise Number of Journals

Observed Frequency (O)	Expected Frequency (E)	(O-E)	$(O-E)^2$	$(O-E)^2E$
12.62%	100%	87.38	7635.26	76.35
6.80%	100%	93.2	8686.24	86.86
9.71%	100%	90.29	8152.28	81.52
9.71%	100%	90.29	8152.28	81.52
3.88%	100%	96.12	9329.05	92.39
11.65%	100%	38.35	7805.72	78.06
7.77%	100%	92.23	8506.37	85.06
10.67%	100%	89.33	7979.84	79.79
6.80%	100%	93.2	8686.24	86.86
10.68%	100%	89.3	7978.06	79.78
9.71%	100%	290.29	8152.28	81.52
				909.71

The Chi-Square test shows that the subject-wise numbers of journals are 909.71.

Dustribution of Users who have come to the Library

Here the total number of users who visited the library from 2001 to 2006 is given month-wise.

The distribution of users who have come to the library is given in the following Table 3.13.

Table 3.13:

Month	2001	2002	2003	2004	2005	2006	Total	%
January	660	812	831	5865	7269	11497	26934	7.55%
February	789	1020	2178	6760	6917	9671	27335	7.68%
March	1256	2405	3700	9430	7174	11760	35725	10.40%
April	1589	2500	4791	3698	5024	6873	24475	6.88%
May	785	1278	3803	337	319	1274	7796	2.19%
June	958	1368	3798	1736	3529	103	13492	3.79%
July	1569	2890	4676	9396	13020	0025	41576	11.69%
August	3250	4586	5865	8264	10254	11217	43436	12.21%
September	2589	4825	6760	9987	10014	11768	45943	12.91%
October	4658	5628	9430	7261	9370	10463	46810	13.16%
November	769	1258	3698	1967	4700	5030	17422	4.90%
December	245	259	337	6179	7314	10595	24929	7.00%
	19117	28829	47867	70880	84904	104276	355873	100%

Table 3.13 shows that the total of 46810 users have visited the library for the six years from 2001 to 2006 during the month of October which comprises of the highest percentage about 13.16 per cent.

Table 3.14: Chi-square Test for user Entry Statistics

Observed Frequency (O)	Expected Frequency (E)	(O-E)	$(O-E)^2$	$(O-E)^2E$
7.55%	100%	-92.45	8547.00	85.47
7.68%	100%	-92.32	8522.98	85.22
10.04%	100%	-89.96	8092.80	80.92
6.88%	100%	-93.12	8671.33	86.71
2.19%	100%	-97.81	9566.79	95.66
3.78%	100%	-96.21	9256.26	92.56
11.69%	100%	-88.31	7798.65	77.98
12.21%	100%	-87.79	7707.08	77.07
12.91%	100%	-87.09	7584.66	75.84
13.16%	100%	-86.84	7541.18	75.41
4.90%	100%	-95.1	9044.01	90.44
7.00%	100%	-93	8649	86.49
				1009.77

The Chi-square test shows that the user entry statistics are 1009.77.

Distribution of Circulation of Books

Here the total number of users who visited the library from 2001 to 2006 is given month-wise.

The distribution of circulation of books is given in the following Table 3.15.

Table 3.15: Year-wise Circulation of Books

Month	2001	2002	2003	2004	2005	2006	Total	%
January	350	658	897	1030	453	3670	7058	6.83%
February	368	589	758	901	216	3391	6223	6.02%
March	1257	1325	1200	1109	735	3703	9329	9.03%
April	450	520	458	691	1168	1597	4884	4.73%
May	150	120	145	127	238	273	1053	1.02%
June	258	247	258	375	311	1192	2641	2.56%
July	1058	1255	1258	1481	2387	3537	10946	10.60%
August	1047	1236	1489	1554	2535	3684	11545	11.18%
September	1258	1489	2123	2152	3193	5418	15633	15.14%
October	1475	1578	2489	2586	4462	5885	18475	17.89%
November	485	489	789	861	1962	1483	6042	5.85%
December	650	789	1288	1346	1268	4118	9459	9.16%
	8779	10265	13152	14213	18928	37951	103288	100%

Table 3.15 shows that the maximum time circulated book during the month of October for about 18475 times for six years (17.89%).

The Chi-square test shows that the year-wise circulations of books are 1010.92.

Distribution of Frequency of Circulation of Books

Here the number of books circulated is given according to the number of times it has been circulated.

The distribution of frequency of circulation is given in the showing Table 3.17.

Table 3.16: Chi-square Test for Year-wise Circulation for Books

Observed Frequency (O)	Expected Frequency (E)	(O-E)	$(O-E)^2$	$\underline{(O-E)^2}E$
6.83%	100%	-93.17	8680.64	86.80
6.02%	100%	-93.98	8832.24	88.32
9.03%	100%	-90.97	8275.74	82.75
4.73%	100%	-95.27	9076.37	90.76
1.02%	100%	-98.98	9797.04	97.97
2.56%	100%	-97.44	9494.55	94.94
10.60%	100%	-89.4	7992.36	79.92
11.18%	100%	-88.82	7888.99	78.88
15.14%	100%	-84.86	7201.21	72.01
17.89%	100%	-82.11	6742.05	67.42
5.85%	100%	-94.15	8864.22	88.64
9.16%	100%	-90.84	8251.90	82.51
				1009.77

Table 3.17: Frequency of Circulation of Books

Number of Times Circulated	Number of Books Circulated	Percentage
1	2	3
1.	2766	32.13%
2.	1465	17.02%
3.	968	1.25%
4.	600	6.97%
5.	529	6.15%
6.	44	5.16%
7.	353	4.10%
8.	269	3.13%
9.	253	2.94%
10.	200	2.31%

Contd...

1	2	3
11.	169	1.96%
12.	161	1.87%
13.	96	1.12%
14.	74	0.86%
15.	57	0.66%
16.	54	0.63%
17.	42	0.49%
18.	21	0.24%
19.	26	0.30%
20.	25	0.29%
21.	8	0.093%
22.	7	0.08%
23.	6	0.07%
24.	4	0.05%
25.	3	0.03%
26.	3	0.0%
27.	2	0.023%
28.	1	0.01%
29.	1	0.01%
30.	1	0.01%
	8608	100%

Total 1.17 shows that 2766 books have been circuited only one time which comprises of 32.03 per cent and 1 book have been circulated 28.29 and 30 times which comprises of 0.01 per cent.

The Chi-square test shows that the frequencies of circulation of books are 27.16.03.

Distribution of Non-Circulated Books

Here the number of books which is not circulated in each subject and the total number of books in each subject is given.

Table 3.18: Chi-square Test for Frequency of Circulation of Books

Observed Frequency (O)	Expected Frequency (E)	(O-E)	$(O-E)^2$	$(O-E)^2E$
32.13%	100%	-67.87	4604.33	46.06
17.02%	100%	-82.98	6885.68	68.85
11.25%	100%	-88.75	7876.56	78.76
6.97%	100%	-93.03	8654.58	86.54
6.15%	100%	-93.85	8807.82	88.07
5.16%	100%	-94.84	8994.62	89.94
4.10%	100%	-95.9	9196.81	91.96
3.13%	100%	-96.87	9383.79	93.83
2.94%	100%	-97.06	9420.64	94.20
2.32%	100%	-97.68	9541.38	95.41
1.96%	100%	-98.04	9611.84	96.11
1.87%	100%	-98.13	9629.49	96.29
1.12%	100%	-98.88	9777.25	97.77
0.86%	100%	-99.14	9828.73	98.28
0.66%	100%	-99.34	9868.43	98.68
0.63%	100%	-99.37	9874.39	98.74
0.49%	100%	-99.51	9902.24	9.02
0.24%	100%	-99.76	9952.05	99.52
0.30%	100%	-99.7	9940.09	99.40
0.29%	100%	-99.71	9942.08	99.42
0.093%	100%	-99.90	9940.09	99.80
0.08%	100%	-99.92	9942.08	99.84
0.07%	100%	-99.93	9980.70	99.86
0.05%	100%	-99.95	9984.00	99.90
0.03	100%	-99.97	9986.00	99.94
0.003%	100%	-99.97	9990.00	99.94
0.23%	100%	-99.97	9994.00	99.94
0.01%	100%	-99.99	9994.00	99.98
0.01%	100%	-99.99	9994.00	99.98
0.01%	100%	-99.99	9994.00	99.98
				2716.03

The distribution of non circulated books is given in the following Table 3.19.

Table 3.19:

Subject	Number of Non-Circulated Books	Total Number of Books	Percentage
English	782	1514	51.65%
Tamil	2531	4421	57.25%
Economics	801	1222	65.55%
Physical Education	721	1638	44.05%
Computer science	1442	3295	43.76%
Commerce	188	1435	13.10%
Biotechnology	64	295	21.69%

Table 3.19 shows that out of the 2271 books in physics 1576 is non circulated which comprises of percentage of 69.40 per cent.

Table 3.20: Chi-square Test for Number of Non-circulated Books

Observed Frequency (O)	Expected Frequency (E)	(O-E)	$(O-E)^2$	$(O-E)^2E$
51.65%	100%	-48.38	2337.72	23.37
57.25%	100%	-42.75	1827.56	18.27
69.40%	100%	-30.6	936.36	9.3[illegible]
40.62%	100%	-59.38	3525.98	35[illegible]
65.55%	100%	-34.45	1186.80	1[illegible]
44.02%	100%	-55.98	3133.76	[illegible]
51.26%	100%	-48.74	2375.58	[illegible]
43.76%	100%	-56.24	3162.93	[illegible]
13.10%	100%	-86.9	7551.61	[illegible]
56.45%	100%	-43.55	1896.60	[illegible]
21.69%	100%	-78.31	6132.4[illegible]	[illegible]

The Chi-square test shows that the numbers of non-circulated books are 340.60.

Findings, Conclusions and Suggestion for Further Research

Findings

The UG Students of all three years is and that of PG Diploma students is 600 of that the percentage is highest case of I year UG of about 34.27 per cent and same is in case of PG Students which is 47 per cent.

There are 19 Teaching staff and 20 Non-teaching staff. It also shows that the numbers of users are more in the other category of Non-teaching staff of about 10 and with regard to teaching staff of computer science department of about 9.

In the year 1998 the books acquired were 2043 (11.37%) which is the lowest and that of in the year 2001 the books acquired were 3820 (2.26%) which is the highest.

The total collection of 27331 books, the book which belong bject Tamil is more in number and has the percentage of 16.18 per cent and self development books are lowest r of about 38 and has the percentage of 014 per cent.

are 90 Indian Journals, 13 foreign Journals of 103 prises of highest percentage of about 50.74 per iodicals. It also shows that there are 183 Indian d 20 foreign periodicals.

ollection of 103 journals, the journals which English is more in number and has the t 12.62 per cent and Biochemistry journals r and has the percentage of 3.88 per cent.

10 users has visited the library for the 006 during the month of October which percentage of 13.16 per cent.

sers has visited the library for six during the month of may which centage of about 2.19 per cent.

has been circulated from 2001 ctober which comprises of the

highest percentage of about 17.89 per cent. That the total of 1053 books has been circulated from 2001 to 2006 during the month of may which comprises of the lowest percentage of about 1.02 per cent.

There are 2766 books has been circulated only one time which comprises of 32.13 per cent and 1 book have been circulated 28, 29, 30 times which comprises of 0.01 per cent.

There are 2271 books in physics 1576 is non circulated which comprises of the percentage if 69.40 per cent. The 1435 books in commerce 188 is non circulated which comprises of the percentage of 13.10 per cent.

Collection Development

College library should frame a book selection policy and also from a library committee for procurement of collections.

Collection of latest edition, text book of various authors, recent journals and magazines to be subscribed. General knowledge and competitive exam books to also be included.

Various database to be purchased and e-journals to be subscribed.

Library Publicity

The Library has to provide wide publicity to the use community about its collection, services, facilities etc. Th only user will be get awareness about the library.

Steps of Cultivate Reading Habits

College libraries should organize programmes finding competitions and similar other programmes the library building. Display of posters, provision of lecturers, library orientation and library user ed programmes should be a regular feature.

Performance Evaluation

Evaluation of every serviced is crucial to gagu it performs and 'Satisfies the demands placed u user'.

College libraries should evaluate their services for judicious allocation of their scare resources and also to know how far they are achieving the goals and performing efficiently and effectively.

Suggestion for Further Research

This is the first study at this college library. How efficient was the collection of the library and how for the collections (books) are effectively utilized to be studied. More similar study about the efficient utilization of the periodicals can also be done in future.

REFERENCES

Anwar, Mumtaz A. Education of user Information, *International Library Review*, 13,1981, pp. 365-383.

Beal, C "Studying Public Information Needs" *Journals of Librurianship* 11, 1979, pp. 130-151.

...rsingh, R.K. and M. Mahapatra, "Current Information Needs and ...heir Providers among the Literatres and Literates: A Comparative ...dy in a Semi-urban Community, "XV all India Conference of ...IC, Bangalore, Dec. 26-29, 1985, pp. 137-49.

... Information: Problems and Prospects in India", Herald of ...Science 26.3-4, 1987, pp. 213-17.

... What Happens with Users? INICAE, Vol. 2,(1) 1983, p. 2.

Resource Management in Academic Libraries

Objectives

In this unit will be able to understand the:

1. Meaning, scope and responsibilities of management.
2. Methods of financial estimation, budgets and management of library finance.
3. Library finance, library expenditure, accounting and items of expenditure.

INTRODUCTION

Financial management more or less revolved around of funds. Aspects like: financial decision-making and problem-solving were neglected a great deal. Modern financial management emphasises wide utilization of funds and gives greater importance to management decision-making. Financial management is considered as essential and integral part of overall management. An efficient and effective financial management is vital for the sustenance and growth of a library. A library is normally considered a non-profit organization.

An academic library is a services component of its parent body. Being a non-profit organization. It as special obligation to manage its finance in judicious names, Besides library services are becoming increasingly expensive to provide.

Meaning, Scope and Responsibilities

"Financial management is a managerial activity concerned with the planning and controlling of financial resources of an organization".

Scope

An organization performs three important activities these includes: production, finance and marketing. The funds are acquired from the sources. The organization expects to get returns on investments over an appropriate period of time. The funds are used to produce services and products.

Responsibilities

The cultural executive authority of the parent body is responsible for the following:

Procurement of finances, investment of funds and getting the sanction for the budget, the library is generally responsible for the following.

1. Managing of funds appropriately.
2. Spending of funds within a specified period.
3. Preparation of budget to fulfill the objectives and goals.
4. Preparation of a report about financial operations.
5. Maintenance of accounts.

Guidelines

Certain guidelines can be laid down for achieving effective financial management. These guidelines are listed below:

1. Easy and simple methods.
2. Economy in financial matters.
3. Simplicity of procedure.
4. Time table for operations.
5. Adherence to saturatory rules procedures.
6. Flexibility in the framework.

emanating from application of information technology. The changes is getting hastened due to the fact that universities are being asked by the university grants commission to earn money to partly support the educational programmers.

Library Expenditure

Nature of library expenditure of an academic library is governed by certain characteristics of a library is by and large a spending institution. It is a non-profit organization and provides products and services to the academic community. A member usually does not have to pay for these charges. However, for certain services like: inter-library loan/Xerox service searching of data bases etc., and depending on certain other factors one may have to pay a certain amount, which may be lower than the actual cost. An academic library is a growing organization. Generally the number of documents users and staff shall keep on growing. To begin with a library may be small affair with the passage of time. It shall grow. A university library after a few decades can become a large one making huge expenditure.

Money can be earned from the following:

(i) Individual members.

(ii) Institutions/Departments/Colleges to which the member of the library belongs to.

(iii) Out Seders (non-members or special members).

The following are the broad possibilities with regard to levying of charges.

(a) No charges the services and products being fee.

(b) Nominal charges to eliminate non services user or discourage misuse of resources.

(c) Charge made to recover the investment or costs.

(d) Charges made to earn project on, the investment.

Normally speaking academic libraries do not charge for services and products. However, for Xerox service, inter library loan, computer database search, etc. Libraries have been charging at a considerably low level than the actual costs. The users have been willing to pay by and large, In some cases, Teachers are billed against the department/institutions or are paying out of research grants available to them. Under the changed circumstances, soon a stage shall be reached when certain services like: Xerox, microfilming, inter library loan translation, computer database service, etc., shall be charged and the authorities shall pressurize the library to recover the actual costs or investment from users. In some case, it may be the institutions, to which the members belong which may have to pay for the services.

There is no harm in charging from outsiders for services and products at actual costs, In fact, a strong case can be made for charging from them at a higher cost to ear project or to disarrange outsiders. The main argument is that an academic library has no responsibility towards outsiders. Any service product made available to them is to them is to be considered a special favorer of them. In any case the services to them should not be at the cost of the members to where the library is duty bound to serve as a priority basis.

In case, the main aim of a library is to make profile, a separate section or unit can be set up to cater to outsiders. This is the trend in developed countries. As an result the members would have less to complain about. The service to them would not suffer the project can be used to maintain certain service which may not be possible otherwise. Today, the situation is that electronic storage and transmission make it easy enough to circulate costs and recover them. Thus charging from both members and non-member can be better managed.

There is every possibility that is the future many academic libraries in India shall be asked by their authority to earn money to; meet the challenge arising due the growing security of funds. Therefore, academic librarians must start discussing the issues concreting craning of many Hopefully, these discussions shall lead to a national debate on the topic of our deep concern which might help us to auditable solution to the underlying issues. The question that arises is if academic librarians get more involved in earning money from outsiders, the members from the parent body may get neglected. This trend as a kind of a future threat which may be beginning to another the users as well as the authorities, However, this trend will add to the value of information and the work of; of librarians will get greater recognitions and respect from the authority and the users.

Accounting

The financial management of a library has two important aspects, *i.e.*, budgetary planning and accounting. Accounting provides information about the economic health of a library. Such information enables the top management to carry out the following functions:

(i) To appraise performance of Library.

(ii) To decide about resources to be invested in terms of time and money.

(iii) To plan and control the operations of a library.

(iv) To take decisions about the future functioning of a library.

In order to enable the tope management carry out above functions, the currents people prepare the following documents.

(a) Financial statements containing cost information.

(b) Reports on the operations of the organization containing summaries of part events and forecasts of future trends.

Cost Accounting

Cost accounting is the process to obtain according to encyclopedia Britannica "estimates of the costs of producing a product. Provoking a service' performing a function of operating department". The task could be cost a cataloguing a book for answering to a reference question.

The process of cost accounting in a library in represented below:

Input process		**Product/service**		**Benefit/Project/Loss**	
(Cost)	(Cost)	(Cost)	(Cost)	(Money/Money/Money)	(Incorrigible)

Basically, speaking there are two methods a cost accenting. There is historical costing and standard costing or pre determined costing.

Historical costing involves calculations of the cost of a product or service after the some has been completed. In standard costing, the detailed estimating of the cost of product or service is carried at before the some has been completed, where by the expenditure can be controlled during the period the product or service is being processed on completion on the product or service, the actual cost can be compared with the estimated cost. Further, variances are calculated and investigate.

The method of standard cost is more refined and is widely adopted because it is more effective in providing the required control to achieve results. It compares the standard cost; this process enables one to calculate the efficiencies of a given operation. As a consequence the required action can be taken immediately to remedy the situation. The variance is the difference between a standard cost or budgeted amount and the actual cost.

Budgetary control and standard costing are comparable systems of cost accounting. Both are pre-determined budgetary control is concerned with comparison of the estimated and actual cost of a library. But standard costing deals with comparison of estimated and actual costs of producing a products or service both are use full aids in controlling costs.

Purposes of Cost Accounting

The purposes of cost accounting are given below:

(a) To estimate expenditure for such function, service section/department.

(*b*) To estimate expenditure for formulation of budget.

(*c*) To fix prices to be charged for various service/products.

(*d*) To control library operations through study of cost of in put and value of out put.

(*e*) To compare costs to measure efficiency.

(*f*) To determine productivity of staff as individuals and groups.

(*g*) To ensure optimal utilization of resources.

(*h*) To help a decision-maker to arrive at correct decision-maker to arrive at correct decision-making.

Cost Effectiveness and Cost benefit Analysis

Vickery has suggested three ways of assessing performances of a system as given below:

(*a*) In the economic efficiency of a system, *i.e.*, the degree to which it minimizes costs in achieving an objective.

(*b*) The effectiveness of the system, *i.e.*, the degree to which it achieves its stated objectives.

(*c*) The value of the system being the degree to which the system contributes to user needs.

Items of Expenditure

Major Items of Expenditures are:

(*a*) *Staff salaries and related charges*: This is the largest budget item in all units and often accounts for over half the total expenditure.

(*b*) *Purchase of documents:* This is the second largest item though it occasionally all too rarely exceeds staff costs.

(*c*) Expenditure on processing (use of the computer, production of bulletins, etc.)

(*d*) Supplies.

(*e*) Equipments (amortization, servicing and replacement).

(*f*) Premises (only significant for large units).

(*g*) General overheads (electricity, clearing, etc.)

(h) *Expenditure on sub-contracting*: This item can be quite important if certain functions (computer processing; are performed by other organizations or if certain jobs (elaboration of a thesaurus) are contracted out.

Methods of Financial Estimation

There are different methods used for working out financial outlay of library. The following are the three methods of finding out the finance required for providing satisfactory library service. These are described in brief;

Propotion Method

In this method, a minimum amount per head of population is fixed and financial estimates are prepared. This type of estimate can be used for public libraries, where the literate persons or adults served is taken into consideration.

In case of University and College libraries, the UGC Library Committee way back in 1957 suggested for a provision of Rs. 15 per student and Rs. 200 per teacher. Whereas, Kothari Commission suggested for an allocation of Rs. 25 per student and Rs. 300 per teacher.

Population Method

In this method a certain proportion of the general budget of a state or institution is recommended for providing library service.

In India standards have been suggested for Public Library Finance. Dr. S.R. Rang Nathan suggested that either 10 per cent of the education budget of a Local/State/Federal Government as the case may should be earmarked for Public Library purpose.

Method of Details

Another method of finding out the financial requirements of a library is called the Method of Details. It implies that all items of expenditure are accounted for while preparing financial estimates for a library. These items, besides others, include: salaries/wages, regarding materials-books, periodicals and newspapers and other kindred materials; binding and repairing heading, cooling and lighting; rents and interest; posts, telegraphs and telephones; and stationery and other contingent and miscellaneous items.

Budget

A budget is an estimation of probable income and expenditure for the ensuring year. In other words, it may be described as a statement of revenue and expenditure for a given period, usually one year. In a way, it is a planned estimation of expenditure within the available income. In the absence of such planning in the financial aspects, it is not possible to spend money in a productive way. It is always essential to identify the things. Which are most necessary out of the list of requirements?

The term budget has been defined in various ways:

(i) A budget is not only a financial plan, but also a forecast guide, cost summer of operation, and historical record and it is also a basis for the formulation of future policy.

(ii) A plan of the amount of money available required, as assigned to a particular purpose.

(iii) A budget is a financial statement of the estimated revenues and expenditures for a given period of time.

(v) A statement of the financial position of a sovereign body for a definite period of time based on detailed estimates of planned or expected expenditure during the period and proposal for financing them.

(vi) A plan for the co-ordination of resources and expenditures covering a definite period of time.

Objectives of Budgeting

The Objectives in preparing a budget are:

(a) To serve as basic financial control mechanism.

(b) To serve as a plan for the efficient and effective co-ordination of resources and expenditures during a particular period of time.

(c) To present a statement of estimated revenues and expenditures, financial situation for a given period of time.

(d) To present details regarding the services those are to be given at a future date.

(e) To serve as a device for evaluating results.

(f) To serve as a tool for the management.

(g) To form the basis for the formulation of future policy.

(h) To serve as a forecast, of the means of carrying the plan into effect, a current guide, cost summary of operations, etc.

Purpose and Funcations of Budgeting

For scientific maintenance of library it is essential to prepare an annual budget. It is a comprehensive document containing the details estimation of and the plans for the financial transaction, which are needed for an organization to carry out its programme effectively during a fiscal period. Budgeting can have positive impact a motivation and moral of staff.

It helps to co-ordinate the entire activities of the organization. It helps to learn from the budget period is over, the librarian can analyse to find out the mistakes and takes steps to avoid in further.

Budget Serves as a Means for Evaluation

Fredrick C. Mosher emphasis the important of budget for the following reasons:

(i) Provides a basis for examining the total rate of the government and its cost in relation on to the private sector of the economy and thus for tailoring the governmental programme to the society and the economy as a whole.

(j) It brings about a regular periodic, reconsideration and revaluation of purposes and objectives of an institution.

(k) It provides the legal basis for the expenditures of funds.

(*l*) Provides the framework for the public accounts and fiscal accountability.

(*m*) Facilitates a comparative evolution of different purposes and programmers in relation to each other and in relation to their relative cost.

(*n*) Provides a periodic link among the administrative organization, the executive the congress and segments of the public sectors and thus an important basis of the democratic information of governmental actives.

Preparation of Budget

Budget is not prepared with in a day or more oral discussion, but it is continuous Job. All requirements and policy decisions, which are taken from time during the year, are in corporate in to an annual estimate. Usually University budget is prepared by or under the direction of the Librarian. Wilson and Tauber suggest 3 ways in which a librarian can prepare budgetary estimates, the following three ways be adopted to prepare library budget.

1. By comparisons with past expenditure.
2. By budgeting in accordance with the work programme.
3. By using widely accepted standard and norms.

Types of Budget

There are many types of budget they are as follows:

- Performance budget.
- Programme budget.
- Formula budget.
- Unit cost budget.
- Lump sum budget.
- 1 On what budget.
- Capital budget.
- Zero base budget.
- Site budget.

Planning and Programming Budget

(a) *Programme budget*: Programme budgeting is based upon the provision of library services rather than individual items or expenditures. It allocates money to services of programme having preciously explored different means to providing services. Which have been identified as needed by the library article. It is focused on the activities and the funds are to be reserved for programmes or services and the library plans to provide. Hence the budget is prepared on the basis of the cost programme.

(b) *Line item budget:* It divides expenditures into broad categories such as: salaries, equipments materials, maintenance, capital and miscellaneous. There are subdivisions within these categories.

Advantages of Lines item Budget

1. Budgeting by organizational unit and object is consistent with the lines of authorities and responsibility in organizational units.
2. This format offers simplicity, ease of preparation, and Recognition by all involved in the budget development process.

(c) *Formula budget*: It allocates the funds to various items on the basis of their assumed relationship, which are important to the services to be rendered. In this type of Formula budgeting, one can only determine the amount the library should get and not how it should be spent. This method of estimation is helpful in an organization where per capita method of financial estimate is one type of formula budgeting. Formula budget users some predetermined standards for allocation of monitory resources such on approach have been adopted by several large library system, with a hope that once the criteria have been established, they can be applied to all units within the library system.

(d) *Organizational unity:* Organizational Unity is pre-requisite for the smooth functioning of any institution. Unity and co-ordination can be better achieved only when there is proper control from above.

(e) *Flexibility:* Financial management should be flexible. Then only it can be successful in times of emergency and crises. But this does not mean that it should take undue advantage of its flexible nature.

(f) *Regularity and fore sightedness:* Financial management should have a typical timetable. This facilitates and advance thinking and advance preparation. It should be borne in mind that besides the need of today, the need of tomorrow should also be in view.

(g) *Legal working:* Legal working of an every organization is extremely necessary to keep it an the right track. Legal working means according to the rules passed by the legislature. This type of working is possible is only when there is financial control.

Conclusion

Finance is the soul to every organization including library also, finance is very important. To get finance to the library mobilization of resource is very important, and also managing these finance is very essential to manage these finance budget and budgeting techniques is very essential to the organization.

Library and Information Science in Digital Library Education

ABSTRACT

This paper identifies the 'state of the art' in digital library education in Library and Information Science programmes, by identifying the readings that are assigned in digital library courses and the topics of these readings. The most frequently-assigned readings are identified at multiple units of analysis, as are the topics on which readings are most frequently assigned. While no core set of readings emerged, there was significant consensus on the authors to be included in digital library course reading assignments, as well as the topics to be covered. Implications for the range of assigned readings and topics for digital library education in library science education are discussed.

Keywords: Research, Previous work, Methodology, Analysis of the assigned readings, Topics in digital libraries, Most frequently assigned books, Most frequently assigned journal articles, Most frequently assigned authors, Distribution of readings across topics.

INTRODUCTION

Hundreds of millions of dollars have been invested in digital library (DL) research since the early 1990s. Much of this research has addressed how DLs can aid education, but there has been no parallel investment in supporting teaching and learning about DLs. Such research investment is of ongoing importance in the United States and other nations (*e.g.*, Australia, China, India, Japan, and many European nations) where significant DL development is being undertaken. Without investment in education related to DLs, we face a future with many digital libraries, but few digital librarians to ensure their success. We run the risk of developers of digital library systems building software that is seriously flawed-since they will not be aware of crucial requirements, efficient and effective techniques for implementation, or key ingredients of success. End users already face a confusing situation where their ability to work with useful information is limited by failures of usability and interoperability. Sponsors of some early digital libraries now wonder about their sustainability, or are concerned about their long-term viability with regard to digital preservation. Those involved in requirements analysis, design, development, management, and utilization of many types of related advanced information systems also face similar problems, which might be avoided with the help of those who have had formal training regarding DLs.

There are, however, currently no formal degree programmes in digital librarianship. A few Library and Information Science (LIS) and Computer Science (CS) programmes offer specific courses on DLs, and a small number of LIS programmes have begun offering certificate programmes in digital librarianship. There is, however, little agreement as to the content and scope of these courses and programmes, and little coordination between institutions. While the Computing Curriculum 2001 (Joint Task Force, 2001), a collaborative effort of ACM and IEEE-CS to define curricula for CS and related programmes, includes DLs as one of fourteen knowledge modules under Information Management, no further work has been supported to develop a DL curriculum for CS beyond the brief CC2001 description.

Research Question

This paper is an attempt to identify the state of the art in DL education in LIS programmes. The authors are currently working on a similar investigation of CS programmes, and plan a future paper on that topic and comparisons between LIS and CS curricula. The present paper, however, is the first step in an effort to identify how the topic of DLs is being taught in LIS programmes. This investigation was guided by the following specific research questions:

1. What readings are assigned in courses on digital libraries in Library and Information Science programmes? Is there a core group of readings?
2. What is the distribution of readings among the various topics in these courses?

Previous Work

Library and Information Science has always been a field concerned with the education of future librarians, and, like many professions, with the integration of research with practice in the field and in the classroom. Consequently, there has been a small but steady stream of studies of LIS curricula over the years. Many of these studies are concerned with the subtopics addressed in LIS courses on various subjects. Many subject areas in LIS programmes have been studied in this way: bibliographic instruction (Larson and Meltzer, 1987), business information (White, 2004), information technology (He, 1999), the economics of information (Weech, 1994), and popular culture (Moran, 1985), to name a few, as well as programmes' core courses (Irwin, 2002). None of the existing studies of LIS curriculum or syllabus, however, have been concerned with courses on DLs. Most of these studies simply list the topics addressed in courses. This is useful information for identifying the scope of what is taught about a subject in LIS, but does not provide more specific information about which topics may be considered to be more or less important. Only White (2004) goes farther, and provides the number of courses in which topics are addressed.

Further, none of these studies reports on the specific readings that are assigned in these courses to address these topics. Only a few studies achieve this level of detail: Joudrey (2002) reports on the textbooks and Chan (1987) reports on both the textbooks and supplementary readings used in courses that address cataloging and classification. Nicholson (2005) reports on the authors and readings assigned in courses on generalized search skills. Larsen (1979) reports on the reference sources introduced in basic reference courses, though not the textbooks or the supplementary readings assigned in these courses.

Methodology

Identification of Courses and Collection of Syllabus

The methods for this study were derived from those used by Joudrey (2002) and Nicholson (2005). The list of course offerings in LIS programmes was viewed on the open web, and courses on the topic of DLs were identified based on their titles and descriptions. Syllabus were collected from courses in which the phrase 'Digital Library' or 'Digital Libraries' were used in either the course title or short catalog description. Syllabus was collected from the open web, as many programmes' websites have links to course syllabus and many instructors have links to the syllabi of courses that they teach. Where syllabuses were not available on the web, the most recent instructor of the course was contacted by email or telephone and asked for a copy of the syllabus. Where no instructor was listed on the programme's website, the programme's main office was contacted. Only the syllabus from the most recent semester in which the course was offered was collected. Thus, only one syllabus per course was considered.

All courses in LIS programmes to a certain extent address DL-related topics, as DLs are at the intersection of most or arguably all of the topics that are addressed in modern library science education. For example, classification and information retrieval are both critical to digital libraries, but no syllabi were collected for courses specifically on these topics. Limiting the collected syllabi to those courses that explicitly use the phrase 'Digital Library' or 'Digital Libraries' was a somewhat arbitrary decision, but it was necessary in order that this study not explode to be an analysis of entire LIS curricula.

While some LIS programmes offer under-graduate majors or minors, syllabus were collected only from programmes and courses at the graduate level. Limiting the scope of the study to graduate programmes enabled the authors to utilize a pre-existing list of graduate programmes of acknowledged quality: the authors utilised the American Library Association's (ALA's) list of Accredited Master's Programmes in Library and Information Studies [1], which contained 56 programmes as of this writing.

Analysis of the Assigned Readings

All readings (*i.e.*, books, book chapters, and articles) listed on the collected syllabus were entered into a citation management database. The way in which readings are listed on syllabus varies greatly: some instructors require students to purchase specific books, and some simply recommend a set of books that students may purchase if they so desire. Some instructors assign a fixed set of readings for each class session and some do not. Some instructors assign entire book chapters and some assign sections of chapters. As a result, this step in the methodology required making some assumptions about the appropriate unit of analysis for identifying readings. In the end, multiple units of analysis were employed: an author, an entire book, an entire journal, and a single journal article. Where an instructor assigned only part of a book chapter or part of a journal article, that assignment was 'rounded up,' as it were, to the larger unit.

Finally, every reading from every syllabus was classified by topic. These topics were those identified by the current authors in their earlier analysis of the Computing Curriculum 2001 (Joint Task Force, 2001). The CC2001 discussion regarding the field of Information Management (Joint Task Force, 2001,

p. 140) provided the starting point for our analysis, with a focus on three core areas (Information models and systems, Database systems, and Data modeling), as well as the four elective areas most related to Library and Information Science (Information storage and retrieval, Hypertext and hypermedia, Multimedia information and systems, and Digital libraries). CC2001 lists a set of topics under each of these areas. The topics suggested by CC2001 were validated through an examination of published papers from DL-related venues (the ACM Conference on Digital Libraries, JCDL, and D-Lib Magazine) (Pomerantz *et al.* 2006). Together, these papers represent a significant portion of the published literature on DLs. Thus the topics into which readings were classified represent the current state of the art and recommended best practices in DL research and education. The result of these preliminary analyses was the list of topics in Fig. 5.1.

The methodology for the current analysis of course readings is similar to that performed by Pomerantz *et al.* (2006) in their analysis of published papers. Every paper in the corpus was assigned to a single topic most closely related to the reading's content focus, from the list of Core Topics in Fig. 5.1. In the process of the topic classification, the topics assigned by the course instructors to the class sessions in which these readings were used were considered, and the original materials were also analyzed to enhance the accuracy of the subject classification. This assignment was performed using methods employed by librarians assigning subject headings: reading the title and abstract, and skimming the actual paper to achieve an understanding of the paper's content. Two members of the research team independently assigned each reading to a topic. These assignments were subsequently reviewed and any differences in categorization were resolved through discussion. This analysis was inductive in the sense that the topic classification scheme was elaborated as new subtopics were identified from the data.

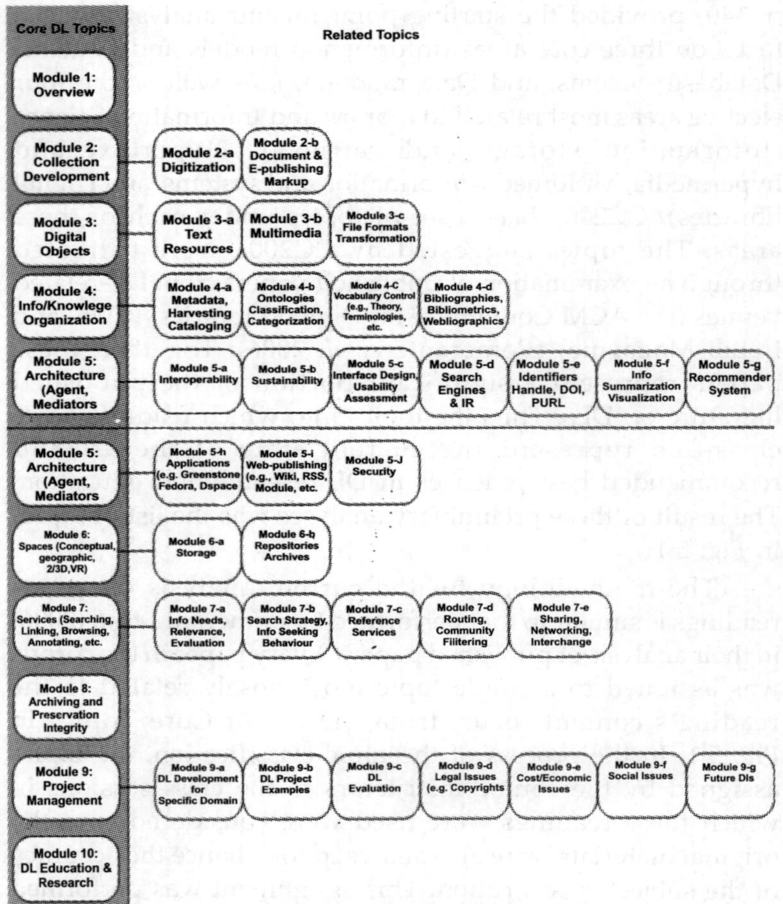

Fig. 5.1: **Topics in Digital Libraries**

(For a larger view of Fig. 5.1)

Results

Most Frequently Assigned Readings

Of the 56 ALA Accredited LIS Master's programmes, 29 programmes offer DL-related courses; thus, 52 per cent of accredited LIS programmes offer courses on DLs. In these 29 programmes, 40 DL-related courses were offered in recent years, between 2003 and 2006. Some of these programmes offer two and even three DL-related courses. In programmes where multiple DL courses are offered, generally one course is a broad-based introductory DL course, and other courses are 'special topics' or clinical courses on specific technologies or services for DLs.

We were able to collect syllabus and their reading lists from 33 courses in 23 programmes. The most recent syllabus collected was from the spring semester 2006, while the oldest syllabus was from fall semester 2003. As mentioned above, syllabus were collected only for the most recent semester in which the course was offered; of the 29 programmes, none offered a DL-related course every semester, and 7 offered a course once a year. The rest of the programmes did not have a regular DL course offering, and many new courses were scheduled to be offered in 2005 and 2006.

Of the 40 courses identified, syllabi for 26 (65%) were available on the open web. Of these 26 syllabus, 6 did not provide the course reading lists. Thus complete course materials were maintained online for only 20 syllabus (50% of courses identified). This percentage is somewhat disappointing, given the courses focus on digital libraries and the fact that 100 per cent of the LIS programmes on the ALA list of Accredited Master's Programmes maintain websites. To obtain those syllabi and reading lists that were not available on the open web, we contacted the instructors of these courses individually via email or telephone.

A total of 1,777 titles for readings were identified in the collected syllabus, where a reading was defined as a book, book chapter, journal, journal article, report, or online source. Of these 1,777 titles, 80 were excluded from this analysis, for a total of 1,697 titles. The 80 titles that were excluded were those books from which only specific chapters were assigned; those individual chapters were included in the analysis. Many readings were assigned in only one course, thus giving the frequency distribution of readings a very long tail. For this reason, only the top few readings of each type are shown in the Table 5.1 to 5.4 below.

Table 5.1 shows the top 5 most frequently assigned book titles in DL courses. These are single - or multiply-authored books, and not edited compilations. The second column shows the number of courses in which the book was assigned. Students in these courses did not necessarily read these books cover-to-cover, however; most often individual chapters were assigned for individual class sessions. Further, these books were not always required for these courses.

Of course, what qualifies as a book is less clear than it once may have been. For example, Arms book, Digital Libraries, was first published in print, and is now available in full text in several locations online. Clearly the print version is a book, but should the online versions also be considered to be books? More confusingly, the work Introduction to Metadata: Pathways to Digital Information [2], edited by Murtha Baca, assigned in several DL courses, is dual-published by the J. Paul Getty Trust, both in print and online. For the purposes of this study, both the examples were categorised as books.

Table 5.2 shows the top 13 most frequently assigned journal articles in DL courses. There appear to be two distinct sets of articles represented among those most frequently assigned: overview articles, such as: Borgman (1999) and Schwartz (2000), and articles on specific topics, such as: Arms, Blanchi and Overly (1997) and Lynch (2005).

Table 5.3 shows the top 13 most frequently assigned journals in DL courses. A total of 121 journals were identified in the collected syllabus. The middle column of Table 5.3 shows the number of courses in which an article from the journal was assigned, and the right hand column shows the number of unique articles from these journals assigned across all courses. These data include two special issues on the topic of digital libraries: ACM Vol. 44 No. 5, May 2001; and Journal of the American Society for Information Science and Technology Vol. 49 No. 11, 1998.

Table 5.1: Most Frequently Assigned Books

Books	# of Assignments	Required in # Courses	Recommended in # Courses	# of Unique Chapters Assigned
Witten, I.H., and Bainbridge, D. (2003). How to Build a Digital Library. San Francisco, CA: Morgan Kaufman Publishers.	13	9	4	9 of 9
Arms, W.Y. (2000). Digital Libraries. Cambridge, MA: The MIT Press.	12	9	3	12 of 14
Borgman, C.L. (2000). From Gutenberg to the Global Information Infrastructure. Cambridge, MA: The MIT Press.	9	6	3	9 of 9
Lesk, M. (2004). Understanding Digital Libraries (Second ed.). San Francisco, CA: Morgan Kaufman Publishers.	8	7	0	14 of 14
Chowdhury, G.G., Chowdhury, S. (2003). Introduction to Digital Libraries. London: Facet.	7	5	2	15 of 15

Table 5.2: Most Frequently Assigned Journal Articles

Articles	# of Assignments
Borgman, C.L. (1999). What are Digital Libraries? Competing Visions. Information Processing and Management, 35(3), 227-243.	9
Bush, V. (1945). As We May Think. The Atlantic Monthly, 101-108.	8
Schwartz, C. (2000). Digital Libraries: An Overview. Journal of Academic Librarianship, 26(6), 385-394.	7
Choudhury, G.S.; Hobbs, B.; M Lorie, Flores, N.E. (2002). A Framework for Evaluating Digital Library Service. D-Lib Magazine July/August 2002. Volume 8 Number 7/8.	5
Levy, D. M. (2000). Digital Libraries and the Problem of Purpose, D-Lib Magazine, 6(1).	5
McCray, A. T., Gallagher, M. E. (2001). Principles for digital library development. Communications of the ACM, 44(5), 48-54.	5
Lynch, C. (2005). Where Do We Go From Here? The Next Decade for Digital Libraries. D-Lib Magazine, 11(7/8).	5
Hill, L.L., Carver, L., Larsgaard, M., Dolin, R., Smith, T.R., Frew, J. (2000). Alexandria digital library: User evaluation studies and system design. Journal of the American Society for Information Science, 51(3), 246-259.	4
Lynch, C. (2002). Digital Collections, Digital Libraries and the Digitization of Cultural Heritage Information. First Monday, 7(5).	4
Lossau, N. (2004). Search Engine Technology and Digital Libraries: Libraries Need to Discover the Academic Internet. D-Lib Magazine, 10(6).	4

The entirety of these special issues (*i.e.*, the entire individual articles in the special issue) was assigned in one of the courses included in this study. Thus, each article in these special issues was counted in the right hand column.

Table 5.3: Most Frequently Assigned Journals

Journal Names	# of Assignments	# of Unique Articles Assigned
D-Lib Magazine	150	85
Communications of the ACM	30	25
Journal of the American Society for Information Science (and Technology)	25	20
First Monday	20	15
Library Trends	15	12
Information Processing and Management	15	8
Computers in Libraries	14	14
Library Journal	12	12
Information Today	10	10
Online	11	11
Journal of Academic Librarianship	10	4
Library Hi Tech	10	8

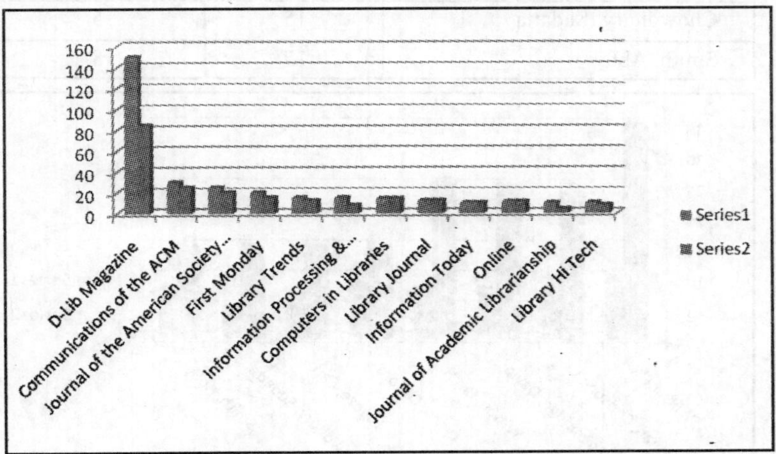

Fig. 5.2

Table 5.4 shows the top 10 most frequently assigned authors in DL courses. An author was counted once for each reading on a syllabus on which his or her name appeared. Authors of all genres of reading were included: authors of books, book chapters, journal articles, etc. This includes multiply-authored works, for which every author was counted once. A total of 949 authors were identified. As in Table 5.3, the middle column of Table 5.4 shows the number of courses in which an article by an author was assigned, and the right hand column shows the number of unique works by these authors assigned across all courses.

Table 5.4: Most Frequently Assigned Authors

Author	# of Assignments	# of Unique Articles Assigned
Arms, Willliam Y.	35	10
Borgman, Christine L.	25	10
Bainbridge, David	25	8
Witten, Ian H.	26	8
Lynch, Clifford	18	9
Lagoze, Carl	15	7
Chowdhury, Sudatta	15	5
Smith, Abby	15	8

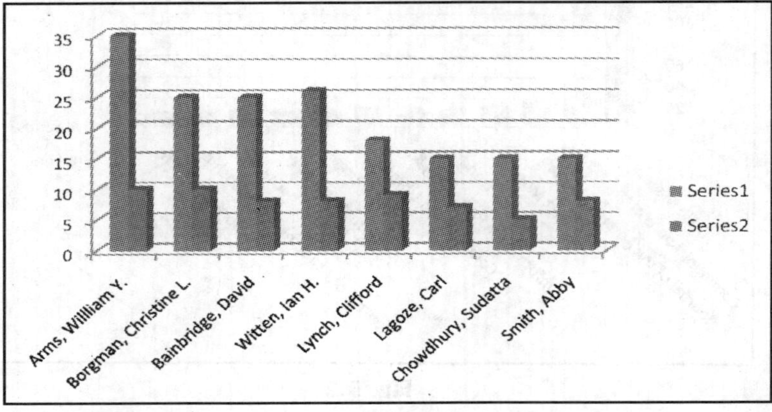

Fig. 5.3

Works with multiple authors present an interesting contrast when looking at authors or at the works themselves. Note that both Ian Witten and David Bainbridge are among the most frequently-assigned authors. Witten and Bainbridge are frequent co-authors; Bainbridge is a co-author of 7 of the 8 publications bearing Witten's name that were identified on DL syllabus, and Witten is a co-author of 7 of the 8 identified publications bearing Bainbridge's name. Note also that Witten and Bainbridge's book, How to Build a Digital Library, is the most-assigned book on DL syllabus.

Classification by Topic

The distribution of readings from DL course syllabi is illustrated in Fig. 5.4. Readings on project management and on DL architectures dominated the syllabus. Other topics that were common across many of the syllabus included collection development, information/knowledge organization, and overviews of the area.

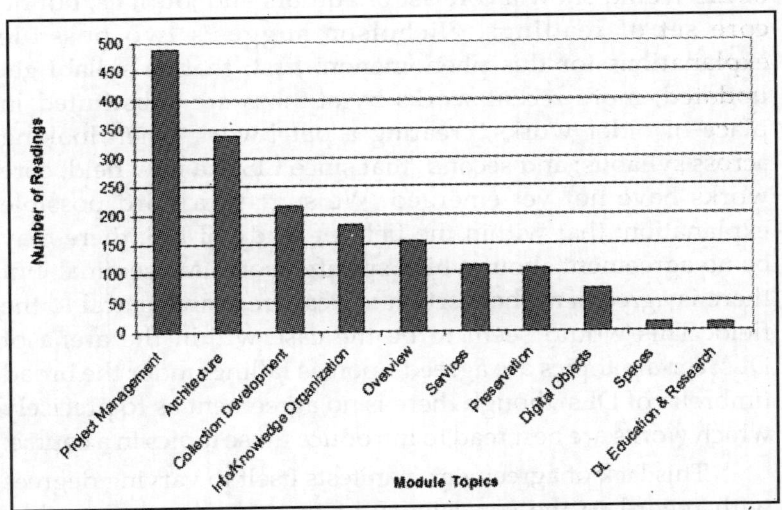

Fig. 5.4: **Distribution of readings across topics**

Undoubtedly all of the courses examined address some DL-related topics through lectures, class discussions, assignments, or some other means, that are not addressed in readings. It is assumed, however, that readings are assigned to address the most important topics in each course and in each class session. Thus, while an analysis of the readings from courses does not provide a complete view of all of the topics addressed in these courses, it does provide a view of the topical highlights, and those which the instructors consider most important.

Discussion

This study found similar results to Nicholson's (2005) findings: there is no core set of readings assigned in DL courses, but there is a core set of authors whose works are assigned. This study also found that there is a core set of journals from which readings are assigned. The authors hypothesize that an analysis of readings in many topical areas of LIS would show a core set of authors and journals, but no core set of readings. Nicholson suggests two possible explanations for this phenomenon: first, that as syllabi get updated, more recent works by authors are substituted in place of older works, creating a patchwork when looking across syllabus; and second, that since LIS is a new field, core works have not yet emerged. We suggest a third possible explanation: that within the field of study of LIS, there may be no agreement about which specific works are seminal, but there is agreement that certain topical areas are central to the field. This would seem to be the case within the arena of DLs: certain topics are agreed upon as falling under the broad umbrella of DLs, though there is no agreement as to precisely which works are best read to introduce those topics in a course.

This lack of agreement manifests itself to varying degrees with regard to the consistency of the readings assigned in courses, by a specific author, from a specific journal, or from a specific book. For example, works by Arms are frequently assigned, and which of Arms' works are assigned is fairly consistent across courses (10 unique works in 36 assignments). On the other hand, works by Marchionini are also frequently assigned, but there is little consistency in these assignments across courses (12 unique works in 15 assignments). As DL curricula continue to evolve, particularly if supported by funded development and dissemination projects (such as: the UNC-VT project described in Pomerantz *et al.* 2006), we may see increases in the consistency of assigned readings across courses; that is, a core set of readings may begin to emerge.

It is in the nature of teaching that courses and course reading lists change over time, both when a course is offered by the same instructor across semesters and when a course is offered by a new instructor. Thus, the set of readings analysed in this study is simply a snapshot of the state of digital library education in the spring 2006 semester. It is possible that different readings could emerge as most frequently assigned if this same study were conducted with syllabus from different semesters. We doubt, however, that this would be the case. We expect that, if this study were replicated, the same authors, books, and journal articles would emerge as the most frequently assigned. The order of the top few most-assigned authors, books, or articles might vary, but the set would likely be consistent.

Whether this expectation is fulfilled or not, it is clear that certain authors, books, and articles at present have a great impact on the teaching of digital library courses in LIS programmes, and possibly will continue to have in the future. In this vein, an interesting issue arises with regard to the use of books in courses, and whether or not a book is 'required' for a course. As is made clear above, whole books and chapters from books are used in many courses in which those books are not required: that is, the instructor does not require that students in the course purchase the book. An instructor may not wish to require that students purchase a book because it is expensive, or an instructor may have created a course pack; there may be any number of reasons why students are not required to purchase a book for a course. Further, even if a book is required in a course, a student still may not purchase it, but instead may take it out of a library. This is especially true for students in LIS programmes: what student knows better to take a book out of a library instead of purchasing it, than a student in library school? Thus a book may be widely used in courses, but still not be widely purchased, at least not by students. And, as students must certainly be a large percentage of the market for the books named above, it may appear to the publishers that these books are not commercial successes, when in fact they are very widely used. Lesk's (2004) book, Understanding Digital Libraries, for example, was enough of a commercial success that the publisher issued a second edition, but not all publishers may be so enlightened. We encourage publishers of books that are widely used in courses to use metrics other than sales to evaluate the success of their books.

As noted earlier, the articles assigned in DL courses tended to fall into two groups: overview articles and articles on specific topics. The overview articles, such as: Borgman (1999) and Schwartz (2000), tended to be assigned near the beginning of the semester, and were presumably assigned as a method for the instructor to introduce the broad topic of DLs. Articles on specific topics, such as: Arms, Blanchi and Overly (1997) and Lynch (2005), were assigned, presumably, as a method for the instructor to introduce that specific topic. Other articles on that topic may exist, but the instructor was more likely to select a familiar article or an article that was likely to provide fodder for class discussion. As courses on DL topics evolve, we are likely to see more convergence on the selection of the overview articles, while there may continue to be variety in those articles used to introduce particular topics.

While publications and conference papers on the topic of Architecture were the most frequently identified in Pomerantz *et al.* (2006), readings on the topic of Project Management were the most frequently assigned in this analysis. Project Management is followed by Architecture and Collection Development. This also differs from the findings in Pomerantz at also, where the topic of Services contained the second greatest number of papers. To a certain extent this is due to the fact that some of the readings that are classified here as Project Management and as Archiving and Preservation Integrity would have been classified as Services in the scheme used in the earlier paper. Perhaps a more important factor, however, is that it would be difficult, if not impossible, to teach a DL course without addressing the topics of Architecture and Collection Development, but papers on these topics are not frequently presented at JCDL or published in D-Library Magazine. Indeed, the topic of Project Management did not even crop up in Pomerantz at also analysis of published papers, but it is another important topic to address in a DL course, particularly in any course that involves a practical assignment to build a DL.

Digital library-related topics are central too much of the curriculum in LIS programmes, and are addressed in many courses across the curriculum. This raises the question of whether, in the long run, courses specifically dedicated to digital libraries have a future. There is, for example, no course in LIS programmes on physical libraries. From a certain point of view, digital libraries are simply environments in which many principles and tools from across the LIS curriculum come together. Time will tell whether courses specifically dedicated to DLs will persist in LIS curricula, or if the topics addressed in DL courses will be integrated into other, more topically focused courses across LIS curricula. Given the spread of DLs over the past decade and a half, however, the authors predict that DL courses will become more rather than less common.

REFERENCES

1. Pandey, S.K. Sharma: Library and Society. Ess Ess, New Delhi, 1992.
2. Chaturvedi D D: Academic Libraries, Anmol, New Delhi, 1994.
3. Devarajan G: User's Approach in Information in Libraries. Ess, Ess, New Delhi, 1989.
4. Devarajan G: Library and Information user and user Studies. Becon Book, New Delhi, 1995.
5. Anwar, Mumtaz A. Education of user Information, International Library Review, 13, 1981, pp. 365-383.
6. Beal, C 'Studying Public Information Needs' *Journals of Librarianship* 11, 1979, pp. 130-151.
7. "XV all India Conference of IASLIC, Bangalore, Dec. 26-29, 1985, pp. 137-49.
8. "Community Information: Problems and Prospects in India", Herald of Library Science 26.3-4, 1987, pp. 213-17.
9. Curras, Emilia: What Happens with Users? INICAE, Vol. 2,(1) 1983, p. 2. Deshpande, K.S: University Library System in India, New Delhi, Sterling 1985.
10. Kumar, P.S.G.A Students Manual of Library and Information Sciences, New Delhi, BRPC (India).
11. Jefferson, Gerge and Burnett, Smith G.C.K: The College Library, London, Clive Bingley, 1978.
12. Mittal, R.L. Library Administration Theory and practices, 5th ed: New Delhi, Metropolitan. co. Pvt. Ltd. 1983.
13. Wilson, Louis Round and Tauber, Maurice F: The University Library, 2nd ed., New York, Columbia University Press, 1956.
14. Pandey, S.K. Sharma: Library and Society. Ess Ess, New Delhi, 1992.
15. Chaturvedi D D: Academic Libraries, Anmol, New Delhi, 1994.
16. Devarajan G: User's Approach in Information in Libraries. Ess, Ess, New Delhi, 1989.
17. Devarajan G: Library and Information user and user Studies. Becon Book, New Delhi, 1995.

Role of Library Resources in Education

INTRODUCTION

Over the years, many libraries have supported education efforts by providing teaching resources, information and referral services. A more active approach has been taken by libraries offering educational classes or one-to-one tutoring programmes. Many libraries have outreach programmes designed to meet the needs of specific groups of people with limited educational skills. Library resource materials are distributed to the institutionalized, including: those in prisons, hospitals, rehabilitation centers, and group homes for the elderly and disabled.

In addition, some libraries offer programmes for groups at risk for education-related problems. Adolescents have been targeted because lack of education has been associated with other problems including: crime, pregnancy, unemployment, drug and alcohol abuse, and school failure. After-school and summer educational programmes have sought to encourage young people to become employable, contributing members of the community and generally to raise their self-esteem. Strategies have included homework help sessions, peer tutoring, and peer-group reading sessions.

Families have been targeted because lack of education seems to be passed from one generation to the next: children whose parents are functionally uneducated are twice as likely as their peers to be functionally uneducated. In family educational programmes, emphasis is on the parent's role as the child's first teacher. Parents, who may have been inspired to seek education training by concern for their children, are taught interactive language activities for use with infants and young children.

Man's quest for knowledge has led to the creation and accumulation of tremendous amount of information. This quest for knowledge knows no bounds and limits and is never satisfied. It has continued since the dawn of civilization to the modern age. This hard-earned knowledge and information is valuable for the entire mankind and therefore liable to be preserved. With the invention of paper man has been able to convey this knowledge to others by writing books. Thousands of manuscripts have been written by the wise men of the earlier times but many of them were destroyed due to the lack of proper means of preservation.

The development of Science and Technology (S&T) in the last two centuries has led to an information explosion. Rapid changes have taken place at a great pace. In order to meet the growing needs of users the library system has been greatly improved and upgraded to meet the new challenges. The services offered by libraries have also undergone a great change.

The shape of traditional libraries containing a large number of printed documents is in the process of being transformed to paper less libraries containing a large number of digitized documents. The facilities offered by networking have not left libraries untouched. Modern libraries are not only digitized but networked also. This has led to the creation of virtual libraries *i.e.,* libraries without walls through which the user has access to information at anytime, anywhere in the world by using the modern tools of communications, such as: computers and Internet facilities.

Libraries in the new millennium are leaders in knowledge management. Librarians in universities are innovative in their use of the new information technologies to provide access to a range of multimedia sources. Today's libraries teach students the information handling skills to last a lifetime.

The traditional image of the library as a quiet place of study, housing mostly print collections, is changing. The shifts in education methods, the impact of computer technology, and the diversity of students have caused libraries to organize resources and design services that meet and anticipate the new needs of study and teaching. Libraries organize collections and provide access and services that incorporate changes in teaching, learning and information technologies.

Keywords: Types of Library, Education, Types of library resources, Librarian and library staff duties, The role of libraries in education.

Library

A library is a collection of sources, resources, and services, and the structure in which it is housed; it is organized for use and maintained by a public body, an institution, or a private individual. It can mean the collection itself, the building or room that houses such a collection, or both. The term 'library 'has itself acquired a secondary meaning: 'a collection of useful material for common use.' This sense is used in fields such as: computer science, mathematics, statistics, electronics and biology.

Libraries are defined as organized collection of published and unpublished books and audiovisual materials with the aid of services of staff who are able to provide and interpret such material as required, to meet the informative research, educational and recreational needs of its users. Libraries are regarded as agencies through which sources of information of accumulated knowledge and experiences are selected, acquired, organized, preserved and disseminated to those who need them. Libraries are essential tools in learning at any level. It is the intellectual centre of the society containing records not only the intellectual but also of cultural, economic and social inclination. With the provision of wide variety of information sources, users of libraries are exposed to different information with their respective values. They also give users the opportunity to learn and continue learning throughout their lives.

Libraries are established for the systematic collection, organization, preservation and dissemination of knowledge and information. It is very important for man to preserve and maintain the valuable knowledge and information contained in the books and documents because we want to preserve our knowledge and wisdom for the coming generations. By preserving the documents in a library this knowledge can be made available to others so that they can benefit from it.

Library (institution), collection of books and other informational materials made available to people for reading, study, or reference. The word library comes from liber, the Latin word for 'book.' (Encarta, 2009) However, library collections have almost always contained a variety of materials. Contemporary libraries maintain collections that include not only printed materials such as: manuscripts, books, newspapers, and magazines, but also art reproductions, films, sound and video recordings, maps, photographs, microfiches, CD-ROMs, computer software, online databases, and other media. In addition to maintaining collections within library buildings, modern libraries often feature telecommunications links that provide users with access to information at remote sites.

The central mission of a library is to collect, organize, preserve, and provide access to knowledge and information. In fulfilling this mission, libraries preserve a valuable record of culture that can be passed down to succeeding generations. Libraries are an essential link in this communication between the past, present, and future. Whether the cultural record is contained in books or in electronic formats, libraries ensure that the record is preserved and made available for later use.

Libraries provide people with access to the information they need to work, play, learn, and govern.

People in many professions use library resources to assist them in their work. People also use library resources to gain information about personal interests or to obtain recreational materials such as: films and novels. Students use libraries to supplement and enhance their classroom experiences, to learn skills in locating sources of information, and to develop good reading and study habits. Public officials use libraries to research legislation and public policy issues. One of the most valued of all cultural institutions, the library provides information and services that are essential to learning and progress.

At the elementary stage library is referred to as:

(i) A collection of literacy documents or record kept for reference or borrowing.

(ii) A depository house built to contain books and other materials for reading and studying.

(iii) A collection of standard programmers and subroutines that is stored and available for immediate use.

(iv) A building that houses a collection of books and other materials.

Advanced definitions of library however are as follows:

(i) As a learned institution equipped with treasures of knowledge maintained, organized, and managed by trained personnel to educate the children, men and women continuously and assist in their self-improvement through an effective and prompt dissemination of information embodied in the resources.

(ii) As an enabling factor to obtain spiritual, inspirational, and recreational activities through reading, and therefore the opportunity of interacting with the society's wealth and accumulated knowledge.

(iii) An instrument of self-education, a means of knowledge and factual information, a centre of intellectual recreation, and a beacon of enlightenment that provides accumulated preserved knowledge of civilization which consequently enriches one's mental vision, and dignifies his habit behaivour, character, taste, attitude, conduct, and outlook on life.

(iv) As a place in which literary and artistic materials, such as: books, periodicals newspapers, pamphlets, prints, records, and tapes, are kept for reading, reference, or lending. In a digital sense, a library may be more than a building that houses a collection of books and other materials as the Internet has opened up an avalanche of online and electronic resources for accessing documents on various fields of interest.

(v) As a collection of texts, images, etc., encoded so as to be stored, retrieved, and read by computer.

Libraries have been identified as one of the key elements for open access to information, which is crucial to educational development. Public and institutional collections and services may be intended for use by people who choose not to - or cannot afford to - purchase an extensive collection themselves, who need material no individual can reasonably be expected to have, or who require professional assistance with their research. In addition to providing materials, libraries also provide the services of librarians who are experts at finding and organizing information and at interpreting information needs. Libraries often provide a place of silence for studying.

Types of Library

The scope of a library as an effective aid to study and education is virtually multitudinous. There are different types of libraries, *viz; (a)* Special library; *(b)* Public library and *(c)* Academic library which contribute to education in various different ways.

(a) *Academic library:* They comprise of school libraries at the primary and secondary levels, College libraries, and

University libraries whose prime objective is to meet the academic needs of the particular institution for which it is created to serve. The purpose of a University library differs, in varying degree, from that of a school or college library in that the former adheres extensive and particular emphasis to research projects apart from the curricular needs of the institution. Besides aiding in the studies of children and assisting the teachers in their teaching and periodic research, a school library is primarily concerned to pro-create an urge for reading habit amongst the children who here get a first hand-knowledge to use the library resources most effectively in their future career. This institution serves to build up a strong mental base and character of children.

Research plays a central role in the academic work of students and faculty at colleges and universities. As a result, college and university libraries-also called academic libraries-are often considered the most important resource of an institution of higher education. Because students and faculty at colleges and universities may wish to conduct research within any conceivable academic discipline, the collections of academic libraries usually reflect a vast range of interests and formats. Academic libraries range in size from the modest collections found in small liberal arts colleges to the immense collections found at research universities. Research universities maintain some of the largest libraries in the world. Most academic libraries are linked to other libraries in cooperative networks, enabling them to share scarce and little-used materials required for advanced research.

(b) *Public libraries:* This on the other hand is most often called 'people's University', in a democratic society operated for the people by the people that conserves and organizes human knowledge in order to place if freely in the service of the community without any distinction of occupation, creed, class, religion, or ethnicity. It is a university of the people since it is maintained and financed by the people of the community who freely throng in this institution and acquire knowledge that they need in their day to day life.

The scope or command of a public library that meets specific but general requirements of the public thus remains quite broader in its vision. It offers from the other types of libraries in that by offering opportunities of informal self-education, it inculcates reading habit amongst all types of general readers and, as a result, maintains a sizeable collection of newspapers, light literature, *i.e.*, fictions, novels, story books, etc., for recreational studies, and a children's corner equipped with juvenile literature. Among its broad based functions to perform in educating the general public as well as the children, the following ones can be quoted:

(a) It facilitates informal self-education of all people in the community.

(b) Enriches and further develops the subject on which individuals are undertaking formal education.

(c) Creates and further develops civic sense and habits of the citizens.

(d) Supports educational, civic, and cultural activities of groups and organizations.

(e) Encourage wholesome recreation and constructive use of leisure time.

(f) Provides children, young people, men and women opportunity to:

  (i) educate them continuously;

  (ii) keep abreast of progress in all fields of knowledge;

  (iii) maintain freedom of expression and constructively provides a critical attitude to all public issues and world affairs.

(c) *Special library*: A special library, which is concerned with literature of particular subject or group of subjects, in an institution which is created to serve the needs of some working organization, either a company, a research

association or a government department. It is often established to save time which the staff, either executive or research, would otherwise employ searching for information. Essentially, the special library has been historically, and remains today, an integral, functioning unit of the organization needs in order to build, prosper, advance, and achieve its ultimate ends.

Many corporations, private businesses, government agencies, museums, religious institutions, hospitals, associations, and other organizations maintain their own libraries to serve the specialized needs of their employees or members. These libraries are commonly called special libraries, but they may also be called information centers, research centers, or technical libraries. The collections of special libraries depend on the specific needs of the organizations they serve. For example, a law firm may maintain its own library of legal documents for use by its lawyers and staff, while a hospital may operate a library of materials in the health sciences to serve its doctors and nurses. In addition to performing the same functions as other libraries, special libraries evaluate, package, and present information to users in ways designed to increase productivity and add to the efficiency of their parent organization. They achieve these goals by reducing the time that employees spend searching for data and by providing information that facilitates improved decision-making.

The highly specialized libraries do necessarily contain certain amount of materials on bordering or allied subjects for instance, the library of the Institute of Business Administration should include such subjects as economics, statistics, banks and banking, etc., beside the all embracing term 'business and commerce'. The library of Pakistan Institute of Development Economics should again contain materials on accountancy, banking and finance, and statistics, while a library specially concerned with the literature relating to television engineering should contain materials on optics and lighting, beside the primarily concerned term 'electronics'.

This happens so usually in a special library for it aims at making available all the possible related materials on a particular topic chosen by a research scholar for research project.

At a glance a special library which is specialized in a particular field of knowledge has a distinguishing mandate of which are:

1. Periodical literature is of prime importance and forms the major part of the collection.
2. Reports, standards, specification form a considerable quantity.
3. It files information rather than materials which calls for introduction of special techniques (mechanical indexing, information retrieval system, etc.,) for organizations.
4. Information here are up-to-date more than the text books, periodical literature or published reports.
5. It ensures quickest dissemination of information (SDI).

School Libraries

School libraries serve elementary schools, middle schools, junior high schools, and high schools. The main function of a school library is to support various educational programmes and to develop students' skills in locating and using information. Teachers use school libraries to access information needed to develop and support their classroom instruction. Students use the materials in school libraries to perform their class work. School libraries usually maintain collections in a variety of media. In addition to books, magazines, and newspapers, school libraries may contain photographs, films, sound and video recordings, computers, CD-ROMs, games, and maps. Some school libraries contain realia, or real artifacts such as: various types of stones for the study of geology. An increasing number of school libraries have computer labs with computer workstations, software, and Internet connections. Because school libraries often emphasize the variety of media in their collections, they are sometimes referred to as library media centers. Most school libraries further enhance their collections by becoming members of school library networks; this allows them to share resources with libraries in other schools.

Education

Education refers to the process of learning and acquiring information. Education can be divided into two main types: formal learning through an institution such as: a school and self-taught learning or what is often termed life experience. Generally, education is important for learning basic life skills, as well as learning advanced skills that can make a person more attractive in the job market.

Education, system of formal teaching and learning as conducted through schools and other institutions. Levels of education in modern societies can go from preschools to colleges and universities.

Education is not only an instrument of social change but viewed as an investment in the national development. Great educational revolutions achieve great economic evaluations.

Education has the same importance as food and shelter and it is known to be essential to a life of an individual. As food is considered necessary for the health and shelter for the body, education is needed for the mind.

Education is assimilated and disseminated in a variety of ways. The least educated people are also instrumental in the propagation of knowledge ostensibly on the basis of lifelong experiences. Such information and knowledge is also imparted to children in their homes daily; however, a quantum leap in the advancement of knowledge demands well-equipped libraries, not only in universities but also in every educational institution.

Education in the largest sense is any act or experience that has a formative effect on the mind, character, or physical ability of an individual. In its technical sense, education is the process by which society deliberately transmits its accumulated knowledge, skills, and values from one generation to another.

(a) Education is the process by which people learn.

(b) Instruction refers to the facilitating of learning, by a tutor or teacher.

(c) Teaching refers to the actions of an instructor to impart learning to the student.

(d) Learning refers to those who are taught, with a view toward preparing them with specific knowledge, skills, or abilities that can be applied upon completion.

Primary Education

Primary (or elementary) education consists of the first 5-10 years of formal, structured education. In general, primary education consists of six or nine years of schooling starting at the age of five or six, although this varies between, and sometimes within, countries.

Secondary Education

In most contemporary educational systems of the world, secondary education comprises the formal education that occurs during adolescence. Depending on the system, schools for this period, or a part of it, may be called secondary or high schools. The exact meaning of any of these terms varies from one system to another. The exact boundary between primary and secondary education also varies from country to country and even within them, but is generally around the seventh to the tenth year of schooling. Secondary education occurs mainly during the teenage years. The purpose of secondary education can be to give common knowledge, to prepare for higher education or to train directly in a profession.

Tertiary/Higher Education

Tertiary education, also called higher, third stage, or post secondary education, is the non-compulsory educational level that follows the completion of a school providing a secondary education, such as: a high school, secondary school. Tertiary education is normally taken to include undergraduate and postgraduate education, as well as vocational education and training. Universities and colleges are the main institutions that provide tertiary education. Collectively, these are sometimes known as tertiary institutions. Tertiary education generally results in the receipt of certificates, diplomas or academic degrees.

Tertiary education includes teaching, research and social services activities of universities, and within the realm of teaching, it includes both the undergraduate level (sometimes referred to as higher education) and the graduate (or postgraduate) level (sometimes referred to as graduate school). Higher education generally involves work towards a degree-level or foundation degree qualification. Higher education is therefore very important to national development, both as a significant industry in its own right, and as a source of trained and educated personnel for the rest of the economy.

Adult Education

Adult education has become common in many countries. It takes on many forms, ranging from formal class-based learning to self-directed learning and e-learning. Adult Education, all forms of schooling and learning programmes in which adults participate. Unlike other types of education, adult education is defined by the student population rather than by the content or complexity of a learning programme. It includes literacy training, community development, university credit programmes, on-the-job training, and continuing professional education. Programmes vary in organization from casual, incidental learning to formal college credit courses. Institutions offering education to adults include colleges, libraries, museums, social service and government agencies, businesses, and churches.

Alternative Education

Alternative education also known as non-traditional education or educational alternative is a broad term that may be used to refer to all forms of education outside of traditional education (for all age groups and levels of education). This may include not only forms of education designed for students with special needs (ranging from teenage pregnancy to intellectual disability), but also forms of education designed for a general audience and employing alternative educational philosophies and methods.

Distance Education

Methods of instruction that utilize different communications technologies to carry teaching to learners in different places. Distance education programmes enable learners and teachers to interact with each other by means of computers, artificial satellites, telephones, radio or television broadcasting, or other technologies. Instruction conducted through the mail is often referred to as correspondence education, although many educators simply consider this the forerunner to distance education. Distance education is also sometimes called distance learning. While distance learning can refer to either formal or informal learning experiences, distance education refers specifically to formal instruction conducted at a distance by a teacher who plans, guides, and evaluates the learning process.

Vocational Education

Instruction in skills necessary for persons who are preparing to enter the labor force or who need training or retraining in the technology of their occupation. The impact of technology on occupations, the tendency of employers to set higher educational requirements, and the need for employees with specialized training have made vocational preparation imperative. Part-time programmes are essential in order to provide occupational mobility among workers and to overcome the effects of job obsolescence.

Audiovisual Education

Audiovisual Education, planning, preparation, and use of devices and materials that involve sight, sound, or both for educational purposes. Among the devices used are still and motion pictures, filmstrips, television, transparencies, audiotapes, records, teaching machines, computers, and videodiscs. The growth of audiovisual education has reflected developments in both technology and learning theory.

Features of Education

1. *Life long process*: - Process of development from infancy to maturity.
2. *Bipolar process*: - Interplay of educator and education.
3. *Tripler process*: - Interplay of educator, education and social process.
4. *A deliberate process*: - The educator is aware of his aim.
5. *Preserver and Transmitter of heritage*: - The cultural heritage is transmitted from generation to generation.
6. *It is progressive*: - Changes according to the needs and demands of the society.

Purpose/Function of Education

(i) Acquisition of information about the past and present: includes traditional disciplines such as: literature, history, science, mathematics etc.

(ii) Formation of healthy social and/or formal relationships among and between students, teachers, others.

(iii) Capacity/ability to evaluate information and to predict future outcomes (decision-making).

(iv) Capacity/ability to seek out alternative solutions and evaluate them (problem-solving).

(v) Development of mental and physical skills: motor, thinking, communication, social, aesthetic.

(vi) Knowledge of moral practices and ethical standards acceptable by society/culture.

(vii) Capacity/ability to recognize and evaluate different points of view.

(viii) *Respect*: giving and receiving recognition as human beings.

(ix) Indoctrination into the culture.

(x) *Capacity/ability to earn a living*: career education.

(xi) *Sense of well-being*: mental and physical health.

(xii) Capacity/ability to be a good citizen, Capacity/ability to think creatively.

(*xiii*) Cultural appreciation: art, music, humanities.

(*xiv*) Understanding of human relations and motivations.

(*xv*) Acquisition/clarification of values related to the physical environment.

(*xvi*) Acquisition/clarification of personal values.

(*xvii*) Self-realization/self-reflection: awareness of one's abilities and goals, Self-esteem/self-efficacy.

Why do we Need Education?

We need education because it improves a person's knowledge. If a person has a good education, he can have the power to choose the way he can use his knowledge - he could either use it for the good of others or for destruction. Why do we need education? Education is necessary so that one's knowledge into its maximum potential and it makes an individual a true intellectual. Education tells a man on how to make a decision and how to think.

Education is needed for the development of oneself, which is vital for the society. For both individuals and the nations, education is the key to the creation, application and the spread of knowledge, which will result to the improvement of the vibrant and globally aggressive financial systems.

We need education because it is one of the most important systems wherein history of a country, its culture and religion and education is the only way to unite the people and the country.

Education - It's Importance in Life

Education is a process whereby you provide information and communicate with your trainees. Education is in fact essential. Knowledge is power, so to be educated is to be empowered. Education allows individuals to transcend poverty and ignorance, to become independent decision-making members of their society. Modern life is often ruthless and fast-moving; education offers a space wherein we can focus on psychological maturity and being self-reliant. The need for education has not changed since the dawn of history. It is important to concentrate on education for many reasons, including earning knowledge and the recognition of others in the field.

Types of Library Resources

Today's libraries are repositories and access points for print, audio, and visual materials in numerous formats, including maps, prints, documents, microform (microform/microfiche), CDs, cassettes, videotapes, DVDs, videogames, e-books, audio books (microfilm/microfiche), and many other electronic resources. Libraries often provide facilities to access to their electronic resources and the Internet. Modern libraries are increasingly being redefined as places to get unrestricted access to information in many formats and from many sources. They are extending services beyond the physical walls of a building, by providing material accessible by electronic means, and by providing the assistance of librarians in navigating and analyzing tremendous amounts of information with a variety of digital tools.

Because they serve such a diverse range of people, libraries maintain collections that can span the spectrum of human knowledge and opinions. Collections include printed materials such as: reference sets, paperback novels, biographies, children's and young adult literature, histories, newspapers, and magazines. They usually also contain photographs, maps, art reproductions, sound recordings, and video recordings. In addition to print and audiovisual materials, computer workstations with software, CD-ROMs, and connections to information worldwide through the Internet.

These library resources play significant roles in education

(i) Human resources (Librarians/information professionals).

(ii) Physical resources (building, conducive environment for learning and teaching, computer, etc.)

(iii) Library resources (print and electronic instruments).

Librarians and Library Staff

The typical library staff consists of three levels of employees: *(i)* professional librarians, *(ii)* support staff, and *(iii)* Library assistants. The proportion of each of these in any given institution depends on the type of library, its budget, and the types of users it serves. Professional librarians usually constitute the smallest number of a library's employees. In addition to their managerial work, professional librarians assume primary responsibility for providing reference assistance, developing and managing the collections, and overseeing cataloging/classification.

Nonprofessional support staff commonly assumes most of the responsibility for directly serving library users. Their activities include essential functions such as: inputting, coding, and verifying bibliographic and other data; ordering library materials; assisting with catalog development; performing circulation duties such as: checking out books to users; and performing other services vital to the library's daily operation. Library Assistants staff members typically shelve books, perform low-level clerical duties, and carry out other relatively simple but essential tasks.

Different kinds of information can be found in different types of resources.

Primary, Secondary and Tertiary Information

Most information is generally divided into three main categories: Primary, Secondary and Tertiary.

Primary Information

Original sources of information and material that has not been interpreted by anyone other than its creator. They include diaries, letters, autobiographies, interviews, speeches, conference literature, stories, patents, poetry, photographs, drama, sheet music, visual art material and statistics.

Secondary Material

Created from primary material, interpreting original material. They are sources of information that analyze and interpret primary sources. Always produced after the events or primary sources they comment upon. They include: scholarly books, articles in journals, reviews and textbooks.

Tertiary Material

Sources of information that analyze and interpret primary sources. Always produced after the events or primary sources they comment upon and act as a tool in understanding and locating information. They include: scholarly books, articles in journals, reviews, textbooks, databases, subject gateways, dictionaries, bibliographies etc.

(a) Books.
(b) Magazine and newspaper articles.
(c) Journals.
(d) Memoirs and autobiographies.
(e) Interviews.
(f) Speeches.
(g) Documents produced by organization.
(h) Photographs and Images.
(i) Cartoons and advertisements.
(j) Movies, videos, DVDs.
(k) Audio recording.
(l) Public opinion polls.
(m) Fiction.
(n) Research data and Statistics.
(o) Documents produced by government agencies.

Reference Materials

Reference material is a good starting point when looking for information and definitions. Reference material includes: dictionaries, encyclopedia, bibliographies, maps and atlases, yearbooks, handbooks and manuals, directories and competitive books etc.

Textbooks

Textbooks are secondary information resources. They will provide you with a good general understanding of a topic. They will often cover many areas of one more general topic. Textbooks will provide you with a good overview and will interpret relevant primary material.

Journal

A periodical published by an institution or professional society in which researchers write about the results of their work to their peer community. It refers to scholarly publications as opposed to magazines that are considered popular publications. Journal articles are primary information resources. Journals are published on a regular basis. Each journal title focuses on a specific area or discipline. They describe research - the generation of new knowledge - and focus on very specific topics.

Databases

Databases are tertiary sources information. A collection of information that can be accessed and searched through the internet. Databases allow you to search across a range of journal articles from different journals.

Newspapers

Newspapers are primary sources of information. They are an excellent source when looking for current and up-to-date information.

Conference Proceedings

Conference proceedings are primary sources of information and record papers presented at conferences.

Websites

Websites are useful sources of current information and for an overview on a topic.

Subject Gateways

Subject Gateways provide a useful starting point when searching for information on the Internet.

Statistics

Statistics are primary information. They can be very useful for looking at patterns and trends.

Abstract

Short summary of an article or book.

Almanac

Collection of miscellaneous facts and statistics on many subjects.

Bibliography

A list of books and articles consulted, appearing at the end of a book or other text. A list of books and articles on a subject. It could also be referred to a list of books and articles written by a specific author or issued by a specific publisher.

Library Catalogue

A list of materials owned by a library, including: books, magazines and journals, audio-visual materials and other materials.

The Role of Libraries in Education

Education' and 'library' are two inseparable-indivisible concepts, both being fundamentally and syn-chronically related to and co-existent with each other. One cannot be separated from the other, and the existence of one is impossibility without the other. None of them is an end in itself; rather both of them together are a means to an ultimate end. One dies as soon as the other perishes. One survives as long as the other exists. This inter-relation, this co-existence, this dependence of one upon the other have been coming down from the birth of human civilization to the posterity through a process of evolution in accord with varied needs, changes, and circumstances of various stages of human life.

Education is an 'aggregate of all the processes by means of which a person develops abilities, altitudes, and other forms of behaivour positive value in the society in which he lives. It is a 'social process by which people are subjected to the influence of a selected and controlled environment (especially that of the school) so that they may attain social competence and optimum individual development. Education is thus the result of acquired knowledge and the cumulating of observations and experiences, while a library is both the fountain and source, and the protector and storehouse of that knowledge and experience. Education cannot exist alone in the absence of library, and library has no meaning if it cannot impart education. Education is an eye-opener to a human being; it gives him perfect, adequate knowledge, creates civic and rational sense, withdraws him from the subjection of low habits, selfish passions, and ignoble pursuits, and thus educes him from abysmal darkness to limpid and perspicuous enlightenment, while library is an instrument of self-education, a means of knowledge and factual information, a centre of intellectual recreation, and a beacon of enlightenment that provide accumulated-preserved knowledge of civilization which consequently enrich ones mental vision, and dignify his habit, behaivour, character, taste, attitude, conduct, and outlook on life.

Education has been defined as a complex of social processes of acquiring knowledge and experience, formally or otherwise. Education involves the total apparatus used for the development of the individual.

The library enables the individual to obtain spiritual, inspirational, and recreational activity through reading, and therefore the opportunity of interacting with the society's wealth and accumulated knowledge. The library can be seen as an extension of education. Library services are needed to keep the skills that have been acquired through literacy classes alive by the provision of good literature..

Education and Library are two inseparable indivisible concepts, both being fundamentally and synchronically related to and co-existent with each other. One cannot be separated from the other. None of them is an end in itself; rather both of them together are a means to an ultimate end. One dies as soon as the other perishes. One survives as long as the other exists. This inter-relation, co-existence, this dependence of one upon the other have been coming down from the birth of human civilization to the posterity through a process of evolution in accord with varied needs, changes, and circumstances of various stages of human life.

Education cannot exist alone in the absence of library and library has no meaning if it cannot impart education. A Good well equipped library is a sine qua non for the intellectual, moral, and spiritual advancement and elevation of the people of a community. It is an indispensable element of the absolute well being of the citizens and that of the nation at large. People acquire education through certain institutions, schools, agencies, welfare bodies, museums and organizations, and the library is the most outstanding of such institutions. A school, a club, and enterprise of a society can never alone impart education; each of them is dependent upon a library – a centre of wholesome education, and the quencher of thirst for concrete, fathomless, ultimate knowledge!

The concept of education for sustainable development and its relationship with Education for All (EFA) is a new vision of sustainable development programme by UNESCO. In December 2002, resolution 57/254 on the United Nations Decade of Education for sustainable Development (2005-14) was adopted by the UN General Assembly and UNESCO was designated lead agency for the promotion of the Decade (UNESCO, 2002).

Indeed, the establishment of the concept on education for sustainable development and its relationship with Education for All (EFA) the United Nations Literacy Decade (UNLD) and the Millennium Development Goals (MDGs) clearly illustrate that quality education, a goal of the library, is a prerequisite for education for sustainable development at all levels and in all modalities of education . The Educational Policies and plans of UNESCO in the role of education and its development, poverty reduction, the promotion of universal human values and tolerance, and the challenges of new ICTs (library).

A Web definition for Education Development is the process of improving the effectiveness of educational provision through an ongoing review of relevant factors at all levels from teaching techniques and materials to institutional structures and policies, and the provision of mechanisms for progressive change.

While the library is essential to any formal educational system, the resources offered by the library are also required by people engaged in improving their education, whether at the remedial, functional or higher educational level.

A good-well-equipped library is a sine qua non for the intellectual, moral, and spiritual advancement and elevation of the people of a community. It is an indispensable element of the absolute well-being of the citizens and that of the nation at large. People acquire education through certain institutions, schools, agencies, welfare bodies, museums, and organizations, and library is the most outstanding of such institution! A school, a club, an enterprise of a society can never alone impart education; each of them is dependent upon a library-a centre of wholesome education and the quencher of thirst for concrete, fathomless, ultimate knowledge!

Library does not mean merely a collection of books. It is a learned institution equipped with treasures of knowledge maintained, organized, and managed by trained personnel to educate the children, men and women continuously and assist in their self-improvement through an effective and prompt dissemination of information embodied in the resources. A research scholar can never successfully conduct his investigations and researches without the help of a library and a librarian. Librarian, as an 'information officer' or a 'scientific officer' possesses, of necessity, definite subject background and knows best the subject area to be covered by an investigator in his narrow field of the problem in hand that he wants to attack! He is a best teacher to guide him with all existing up-to-date possible sources including various articles in research journals, periodicals, etc., as well as the rare information available in rare books, microfilms, microfiche, manuscripts, and the like. He can guide him most effectively and comprehensively with the bibliographies, indexes, abstracts, data-books and such innumerable reference sources and bibliographical apparatus which the investigator might, otherwise, are unaware of. Here a professionally trained efficient librarian plays a most significant role in the achievement of modern scientific discoveries. The importance of an up-to-date library in the projection of research studies can thus be very scarcely over emphasised.

It is evident that the different types of libraries play a significant role on different styles in educating the citizenry of a nation. The utility of a library in education can at once be felt and generalised particularly when we look into the educational conditions of the poor. The most flagrant aspect of the predicament of the poor people in developing countries (poor countries) is that their children are subjected to woefully inefficient public education. The degree of reading retardation among the children of rejected and oppressed peoples in developing countries is traumatically alarming. This is due to their poverty that culminates in their inability to purchase valuable books and also to bear heavy expenses of tuition fees, etc. With the help of the libraries it may very well lodge a 'war' or campaign against this poverty for which the education has remained handicapped and limited to the people of the upper strata of our society. Libraries make available all the relevant books and other materials almost free of cost, and the children of the poor and the rich alike can derive equal amount of advantages out of this free service that helps in pursuing constructive education.

Libraries render a yeoman service in education through extension services and audio-visual aids, *viz;* story hours, lectures, book exhibitions, displays, book weeks, and motion pictures, newsreels, film strips, music scores, phonorecocds, and the like. These aids save people from the hackneyed monotony of perusing books, and teach them practically on the spot. They are also an aid to mass education of those who cannot read or write. This is of particular importance to the overwhelming illiterate people living in the villages. The traveling libraries are also of particular significance here since they carry the books to those remote areas of villages and towns where education could not thrive due to the absence of reading materials and reading centers.

A library has been the chief conserver of knowledge achieved by men in their intellectual pursuits that helps in generating new ideas and discoveries, while 'education' is an art of making available to each generation the organized knowledge of the past. A library is not, however, merely a conserver of the past events, experiences, and knowledge. 'The preservation of the physical object called the 'book', for example, may not be important in itself. What is important is for the library to transmit to the incoming generations the ideas which the book contains.' Through the instructional staff of the academic institutions the knowledge and ideas conserved by a library are revitalized arid put to use in the education of youth who are to be leaders in society and workers in the field of research, and through the methods of research the students are given an opportunity for independent works, and then the libraries and laboratories become inescapable and vital aids in an Endeavour which is directed toward the expansion of man's fund of knowledge. While the library makes this direct contribution to the advancement of knowledge, it serves as the principal training ground for those who undertake investigations in the fields of science, technology, industry, and the like.

Libraries are information and communication systems. The more complex the society is in its educational requirements the greater its dependence upon library based information services. Specifically, the primary purpose of libraries is as follows:

1. Enable information education opportunities for the citizens in the communities.

2. Enrich the knowledge of individuals in various subject disciplines where they undertake formal education.
3. Provide awareness to meet the information needs of people.
4. Support the educational, civil and cultural activities of groups and organizations.
5. Provide recreational opportunities and encourage constructive use of leisure time.

Libraries in carrying out this role of education can provide necessary materials such as: textbooks, journals, magazines and exercise books related to the curriculum of the existing literacy institutions in the community be it conventional schools or adult classes. In this way, it has assisted in the campaign to make the society a more literate one. Libraries are regarded as the people's university providing and independent decision taking. Libraries attempt to meet a wide varies of readers needs, providing varied information resources such as: text books, journals, literary books and other publications.

The 1994 UNESCO manifesto sees libraries as a living force for a practical demonstration of universal as a lifelong process. Libraries can richly compliment the educational activities by assisting adult in no longer of school age, developing their attitudes, extending the knowledge and by acquiring, needed technical or vocational skills (UNESCO, 1994). In this way, the adult education products would emerge as responsible members of the society.

In carrying out its role, libraries can also train the personnel carrying out the different educational programme in the community. This can be done by the library carrying out seminars. Workshops and conference on the different subject areas of the literacy programmes; so that they can become better at their various fields. Libraries can also carry out their roles as education providers for their community by setting up literacy institutions such as: adult literacy programmes in their community.

Libraries are very important in the life of any nation. If nation must develop, if a nation must achieve possible growth rate per capital income, the majority of the populace must be educated. The most effective method of developing human resources is through education.

Through education, the masses can attain literacy that is a prerequisite for any success in our national development. Libraries provide book and non-book materials to meet the educational needs and support the efforts of the adult's education programmes to help contribute to the growth of a nation. Libraries have vital role to play in decision and policy-making. It is in search of this justification libraries were established.

Library resources continue to play an important role in the education programme in sustaining the diverse forms of cultural expressions. Libraries acquire process, organize and preserve materials, which depict the way of life and experiences from others. Through libraries, the illiterate's class can develop the skills in computer usage in searching for collection. Indexing and abstracting services. The library provide reading and learning materials to help argument lectures notes with facts and with ideas; provide information service, which is an essential element in the communication process. One requires information to communicate effectively.

Libraries can play their role of information by making available journals, newspapers and all other reading materials in the indigenous language so that education will be available at the grassroots.

Library resources provide the information needs of the illiterates that constitute the bulk of the population in the developing countries and unite all who enter its house to partake full in its intellectual activities. The institution serves as the society's memory, standing the same relationship as the human memory does to the individual. The society draws from the libraries in the same way that an individual draws from his memory to meet his varied needs.

In the past few years the Web has had a tremendous effect on the growth of information and the speed of transmission. But the Web is not a library; there is no real organization of information, no archives, filter, or online support. No-one can really be sure what is there and how long it will last, or what is missing. And despite its size, the Web represents only a fraction of the world's knowledge. Libraries however, select and organize print and electronic resources, databases and multimedia for quality, relevance and reliability. Library collections span continents and centuries, and preserve and make available to users a wealth of knowledge.

Libraries are viewed as an important component of education without the library no meaningful educational efforts can be carried out. Generally, education is considered to be the imparting and acquiring of knowledge through teaching and learning, especially at a school or similar institution. Functional education involves skills needed to cope with everyday situations. The importance of the library in educational cannot be over-estimated. Thus the libraries have an essential and close bearing upon the advancement of education and learning at all levels for all the times to come.

Libraries Inspire Education

When individuals of all ages have the opportunity to explore information that matters to them, various forms of education can emerge. Libraries have tools to inspire education of all ages.

(a) They teach skills and strategies individuals need to learn and achieve.

(b) They are partners in education, developing curricula, and integrating resourced into teaching and learning.

(c) They teach the skills individuals need to become effective users of ideas and information.

(d) They seek, select, evaluate, and utilize electronic resources and tools and instruct individuals and educators in how to use them.

(e) Library is the ideal neutral and non threatening environment for learning, formal and informal, to occur.

(f) Libraries have a record of personal service and impartiality.

(g) They readily partner with other learning providers and with other libraries.

(h) They provide public ICT facilities and support.

Libraries are True Places of Opportunity when

- All individuals can strive for and achieve success.
- Quality collections are provided, in print and online, that support educational curriculum and address a variety of learning needs.
- Individuals can develop a love of reading and literature.
- Librarians help individuals explore the world around them through print and electronic media individuals can work individually or in small groups on research and collaborative projects.

Librarian/Information Professionals Role in Education

- They teach skills and strategies individuals need to learn and achieve.
- They are partners in educating individuals, developing curricula, and integrating resources into teaching and learning.
- They teach the skills individuals need to become effective users of ideas and information.
- They seek, select, evaluate, and utilize electronic resources and tools and instruct individuals and educators in how to use them.
- They provide collaborative programmes for reading instruction.
- They select resources to meet the learning needs of all individuals.
- They provide imaginative materials that promote learning motivation.

- They encourage individuals to seek, access, and use information independently.
- They provide for free voluntary reading, individual reading selection and reading guidance
- They provide avenues for achieving set objectives and mission of education.
- Manage information by providing intellectual and physical access to information in print, media, and online resources, either local or web based.
- Collaborate with lecturers, teachers, educators regularly to provide resources and activities for course, unit, and lesson integration.
- Promote reading advocacy by matching students to books in all formats, including print, audio, and e-books.
- Teach information skills, Organize, manage, and maintain a collection of valuable resources.
- Provide resources and activities for individuals that are meaningful now and in the future Share the findings of reading research with educators.
- Maintain a supportive and nurturing environment in the library and network environment to increase individual satisfaction and achievement.

Importance of Library in Education

Library is like a storehouse of knowledge. You will find books in a library in almost all topics, be it history, geography, or even science fiction a library has it all. All schools and colleges have a library. Libraries are as the shrine where all the relics of the ancient saints, full of true virtue, and that without delusion or imposture, are preserved and reposed - Bacon. A library is like the whole world encompassed in one room. Without a library a school will not be complete. It is very essential to the education and school system. Any problem you have any query unanswered you will find it in one of the books stored in the library.

It caters to the knowledge thirsty minds of thousands of people. With the onset and advancement of technologies virtual libraries are created. These types of libraries are present in many colleges.

The role of the library resources in education is to:

- Facilitate the planning and implementation of learning programmes that will equip students with the skills necessary to succeed in a constantly changing social and economic environment. Through resource-based programmes, students acquire skills to collect, critically analyze and organize information, problem-solve and communicate their understandings.
- Provide and promotes quality fiction to develop and sustain in students the habit and enjoyment of reading for pleasure and to enrich students' intellectual, aesthetic, cultural and emotional growth.
- Cater for differences in learning and teaching styles through the provision of and equality of access to, a wide range of materials, fiction and non-fiction, print, audio, video and digital.
- Provide educators with access to relevant curriculum information and professional development materials within and outside the educational system; and opportunities to cooperatively plan implement and evaluate learning programmes which integrate information resources and technologies. (Usoro, 2007).
- A State of literacy may be attained and maintained.
- Maintain a supportive and nurturing environment in the library and network environment to increase individual satisfaction and achievement.
- The individual may continuously improve his knowledge and skills.
- The individual may be made aware of the common citizenship, cultural heritage, and social values, and thus adapt to changing roles in adult life.

- The individual may develop his personality and full potential, widening the range of his perception, interest and skills.
- The library enables the individual to obtain spiritual, inspirational, and recreational activity through reading, and therefore the opportunity of interacting with the society's wealth and accumulated knowledge. The library can be seen as an Integra part of education.
- Giving personal awareness to learners of their rights in the society and to appreciate the social values and be able to change for easy adaptation into the expected roles within the society.
- Enabling the individual to develop its full potentials and widening the range of its perception, interests and skills.
- Library resources help to develop a habit of lifelong learning. Library resources are needed to keep the skills that have been required through education alive. If education is to have a greater share in the molding and building of a happier individual and a better society, the providers of education must go beyond their roles as facilitators to a more practical role of providing library resources for sustaining the newly acquired skills of adult learners.
- Library provision in primary and secondary schools has an impact on student learning.
- Library provision can contribute to academic achievement, particularly in reading literacy, in primary level students. stimulate and guide pupils in all phases of their reading so that they may find increasing enjoyment and satisfaction and may grow in critical judgment and appreciation.
- Provide an opportunity through library experience for boys and girls to develop helpful interests, to make satisfactory personal adjustments, and to acquire desirable social attitudes.

- Help children and young people to become skillful and discriminating users of libraries and of printed and audio-visual materials.
- Libraries are as important as education itself. Library services imply both availability and accessibility of library resources, facilities and services to the user and the willingness and ability of readers to use the facilities and services.
- Individuals need the library for effective learning for lifelong education, the aim of basic education is to equip individual with such knowledge, skill, and attitude that will enable them to:
  1. live meaningful and fulfilling lives.
  2. contribute to the development of the society.
  3. derive maximum social economic and cultural benefits from the society.
  4. discharge their civil obligation.

Inculcating the Habit of Reading

Reading is regarded as one of the most enriching habits for the simple reason that it is not just a hobby or a pass time that entertains you, but it is also an educational activity and hence brings to you a vast reservoir of knowledge. Reading increases the drive for knowledge and inspires people to gain more information. Thus a library is a treasure of valuable books for the people to use and gain from it.

Learning Experience for the Children

A library is a very important aspect in the learning process of children. The extensive genre of children's literature is an essential part of the growing up process. Most of the public libraries are keeping with the times and equipped with facilities like: CDs and even computers.

Reference for School/Colleges

The quintessential library is a boon for the students in schools and colleges. There exist a large number of reference books that provide information about wide ranging subjects are a must for students to understand the concepts in their curriculum. The reference books often provide in depth information about various subjects and thus help in the process of education.

Advice on Important Subjects

There are large number of books that provide advice about various topics like: business, health, travel, food and careers. These books serve as a great source of advice. Many people make it a point to read and go through these books before taking important decisions in their life. Thus libraries are also helpful for people who are looking for information about specific subjects. For example a person who is planning to travel to a particular place would like to read about that destination.

Wholesome Information

A library usually has a good collection of encyclopedia, dictionaries and maps, which are a source of extensive information and references for people. The encyclopedias are a vast source of information about all the topics under the sky. There also exist specialized dictionaries like medical dictionaries, literature dictionaries or business dictionaries, which provide information about specific terms used in specialized fields.

Entertainment and Fun

In addition to the above mentioned points, libraries are also a host to large number of books that are a source of entertainment for us. Fiction books, which include various genres like: comedy, thriller, suspense, horror or drama, are tremendously popular within readers of varying age.groups. Libraries are thus a source of entertainment and education for youngsters as well as adults. A library not only helps to inculcate the habit of reading but inculcates a thirst for knowledge, which is makes a person humble and open to new ideas throughout his/her life.

Conclusion

Libraries are vital institutions, which cannot be separated from education. The provision of libraries is crucial and indispensable to education in a nation. Therefore, whatever is done to improve the quality of education is done to improve the nation. The absence of libraries will have negative effects on education. Therefore, individual learners should be encouraged to use them.

REFERENCES

Importance of libraries in Education Retrieved June 20, 2011, from http:/ / http://ezinearticles.com/?Importance-of-Libraries&id=458166

Role of the School Library Retrieved June 20, 2011, from http:// www.det.wa.edu.au/education/cmis/eval/library/value/val1.htm

Importance of a Library Retrieved June 20, 2011, from http://www.buzzle.com/articles/importance-of-a-library.html

Life Retrieved June 20, 2011, from http://hubpages.com/hub/Education _importance

Teachers mind resources Retrieved June 20, 2011, from http://www.teachersmind.com/Education.html

The role of public libraries in non formal education. Retrieved June 22, 2011, from http://eprints.rclis.org/bitstream/10760/15208/1/ Lila2.pdf

The Role of the Academic Library. Retrieved Adio, Gboyega. The Role of Library in Educational Development.

The Role of Library Services in Adult Literacy Education. Library Philosophy and Practice (eojournal).

Retrieved June 25, 2011, from http://ezinearticles.com/?Importance-of-Libraries&id=458166

The Role of Libraries in Education. Retrieved June 25, 2011, from http:// www.infosciencetoday.org/library-science/the-role-of-libraries-in-education.html

Types of Information Resources. Retrieved June 25, 2011, from ttp:// www.ucd.ie/library/students/information_skills/resources.htmls

Index

****